Black Church Life-Styles

Emmanuel L. McCall
COMPILER

BLACK CHURCH Life-styles

BROADMAN PRESS
Nashville, Tennessee

© Copyright 1986 • **Broadman Press**
All Rights Reserved
4256-65
ISBN: 0-8054-5665-1
Dewey Decimal Classification: 260
Subject Heading: BLACKS-RELIGION // BLACK CHURCHES
Library of Congress Catalog Number: 86-17591
Printed in the United States of America

Unless otherwise stated, all Scripture quotations are from the King James Version of the Bible. Scripture quotations marked GNB are from the *Good News Bible,* the Bible in Today's English Version. Old Testament: Copyright © American Bible Society 1976; New Testament: Copyright © American Bible Society 1966, 1971, 1976. Used by permission.

Library of Congress Cataloging-in-Publication Data

Black church life-styles.

Rev. ed. of: The Black Christian experience / Emmanuel L. McCall, compiler. 1972.
  Bibliography: p.
  Contents: Black church distinctives / Otis Moss, Jr. — Black Baptist church history / Emmanuel L. McCall — Black nurture / Ella Mitchel — [etc.]
  1. Afro-Americans—Religion. I. Black Christian experience. II. Title: Black church lifestyles.
BS563.N4B567 1986   277.3'008996073   86-17591
ISBN 0-8054-5665-1 (pbk.)

Dedication

During the late 1960s and early 1970s, a number of young people were misled into believing that the black church was their enemy, that it was an "Uncle Tom" institution. These accusations were challenged by men and women who believed "the truth must be told." They remembered, they researched, they discussed, they lectured, and they wrote. This book is dedicated to "those who hungered and thirsted for righteousness." May their days be full.
—Emmanuel McCall

Contents

Foreword 9
by Emmanuel L. McCall

1.
Black Church Distinctives 11
Otis Moss, Jr.

2.
Black Baptist Church History 21
Emmanuel L. McCall

3.
Black Nurture 45
Ella Mitchell

4.
Worship in the Black Church 69
Dearing E. King

5.
Black Hymnody 83
Wendel Whalum

6.
Black Preaching 105
Henry H. Mitchell

7.
The Black Church's Outreach 127
W. J. Hodge

8.
Cults in the Black Community 141
Emmanuel L. McCall

9.
The Black Church Renaissance 161
Otis Moss, Jr.

10.
Selected Bibliography on the Black Church 171

Foreword
by Emmanual L. McCall

The first edition of this book appeared in 1972 as *The Black Christian Experience*. The purpose of that edition was to provide a generally comprehensive look at the experiences of Christians of Afro-American descent.

Over a decade later there is still the need to provide an easily read interpretation of black church life-styles. To this end we have revised *The Black Christian Experience*. The new edition rearranges, updates, and expands the original material.

One of the lessons learned since 1972 is that there is no such thing as *the* black Christian experience. There are varieties of experiences among black Christians. Those experiences are multiplied according to geography, customs, traditions, life-styles, preferences, and heritage.

This book does not attempt to be totally inclusive of all that can be spoken and written about black religious experiences. It is not intended as a classroom text, although it may be used as such. *Black Church Life-Styles* does attempt to provide the reader with an introductory approach to an appreciation of black heritages, especially from the perspectives of Baptists. For those who wish to read further, a select bibliography concludes the book.

Emmanuel L. McCall, Sr.

1
Black Church Distinctives
Otis Moss, Jr.

(*Editor's note:* This chapter by Otis Moss remains essentially as it was written in 1971 because its relevance is unchanged.)

For better or for worse in the North American section of the Western Hemisphere, we do have what can be relatively designated as the black church and the white church. The black church is the product of one of the agonies in Christian history. There are four compelling agonies in Christendom. These are: war, anti-Semitism, exploitative kinds of capitalism, and racism.

All of these are serious challenges to the Christian faith. The issue of race, however, has caused the American church to lose much respect in the modern world. It is at this point that the black church might be referred to as the remnant church, maybe the last creative force and perhaps the last, best hope for a redeeming faith in our time. But I use the word *maybe* because no system of theology has the last word. God has the last word. Therefore, no matter what I might think, no matter what C. Eric Lincoln, James Cone, or any others of giving interpretations to the popular theme of blackness may think, we must keep in mind is that we do not have the last word. We never know when and where God might appear and do the impossible. Therefore, it is dangerous for any of us to conclude, "This is it." God is still the Alpha and Omega of history.

Let me make a few statements here. The concept of "soul" and "soul music" has its roots in the black church. Whether it is the late

Mahalia Jackson or Diana Ross; whether it is Lionel Richey or Stevie Wonder; whether it is William Warfield or Kool and the Gang, soul music has its roots in the black church.

These popular vocalists and musicians today who are gathering a fortune are really indebted to the black church. I don't know if they have paid their dues lately or not, but they got it "at home" and "down home." When I listen to James Brown, I am reminded of the singing of Deacon Will Truett at the Old Mount Olive Baptist Church in Troupe County, Georgia. The mailing address was La Grange, but that was a long way from Old Mount Olive.

It is true to history, then, to say that the agonies of racism are the birth pangs of the black church. The black church is an indictment and a commitment in Western culture.

This thing we call the black church (and this is a limited definition) is really "that Christian fellowship whose origin or establishment, administration, function, life, order, and structure are exclusively in the hands of black people." In a sense we are talking about a relative and limited fellowship. These congregations or fellowships are primarily black Baptists founded as early as 1776 and a few years before: the AMEs (African Methodists Episcopals) 1816 and the AME Zion, 1821. The CME (Colored Methodist Episcopal) was organized by whites to keep blacks out of the white church. That's why they were called Colored Methodists beginning in 1870, but in 1957 changed their name to Christian Methodist. So they were Colored Methodists historically and Christian Methodists by legislation.

In addition to the classical denominations among black people there are also the sects, the cults, the holiness, and other church bodies which have been numerous in the urban culture. In 1807 an African Presbyterian Church was founded. In 1818 the Black Episcopal Church was organized. In 1829 a Black Congregational Church was founded. But the Baptists and the Methodists had the greatest appeal to the masses of black people in North America, and there are good reasons why.

Black Church Distinctives   13

In the highly sophisticated, liturgical church, everything was organized years before they got to that moment. The order of worship—the prayers and everything else—was all organized years before the hour of worship or the experience of worship. The prayers were all written out in the book. The slaves could not carry a prayer book around in their hip pockets out in the cotton fields, in order to say: "Lord, bless the queen of England and all of her cabinet. Bless the government and the Parliament." They didn't have the time to go through all of that. In fact, they were unable to read.

But as the sun made its journey, or as the earth made its revolution, they looked toward the setting of the sun and said:

> This evening, our Heavenly Father, it's once more and again that this your humble servant, knee bent and body bowed, one more time. And as I bow, I want to thank you for my last night's lying down. I want to thank you for a guardian angel that you sent to watch over me all night long while I slumbered and slept. I want to thank you because you touched me with a finger of love this morning, and woke me up on due time. I yet have the activity of my limbs, and my tongue was not cleaved to the roof of my mouth. I was yet left in a gospel and a Bible-reading country. . . .

Then they looked around at a mean boss man and said: "where mens and womens won't do right."

The black church was founded in slavery, through a certain kind of freedom that was invisibly communicated from God to slaves which the slave master could not catch. While we were, in terms of geography, a long way removed from "Jerusalem," God planted in our souls the seeds of a "new Jerusalem."

The early establishment of the classical black church was by slaves, ex-slaves, and some free black people during the era of slavery. This is why some of these churches are called *African* Methodist Episcopal, *African* Methodist Episcopal Zion, First *African* Baptist. Of course, some cultural changes took place. I will not take the time to delve into this, but it would be interesting for someone to get some background on the stages we went through. There was the African stage, the colored stage, the Negro stage, and now back to the black stage.

When our memories were yet closed to the coasts of West Africa, we yet had not only an African culture but even in our conversation, in our own tradition, we had a living memory of Africa. But then the islands of the sea were infused in the slavery experience causing some people to say, "We are from the island, we are not Africans," and they were right. So there was a decision that maybe "colored" was more inclusive, for that would include Africa and the islands of the seas. Somebody else said, "We are neither *African* nor *colored*. We are *Negro*." Today we say we are just *black*.

Are Black and White Churches Different?

The distinct difference between the black church and the white church must be remembered. Even though we get some literature from them once in a while, there is a difference.

What are some of the differences? In the first place the black church is the church of the oppressed, and the white church is the church of the oppressor. Now it isn't to say that everybody identified with the white church is by the fact of identification an oppressor, but it is the institution of the oppressor. There is a difference. You see, the songs of the Hebrews in Babylon will always be different from those of the Babylonians of Babylon. The songs of the people *in the world* and yet not *of the world* will always be different from the songs of the people of the world. The Babylonian could sing one kind of song, but the Hebrews said:

> By the rivers of Babylon, there we sat down, yea, we wept, when we remembered Zion. We hanged our harps upon the willows in the midst thereof. For there they that carried us away captive required of us a song; and they that wasted us required of us mirth, saying, Sing us one of the songs of Zion. How shall we sing the Lord's song in a strange

land? If I forget thee, O Jerusalem, let my right hand forget her cunning. If I do not remember thee, let my tongue cleave to the roof of my mouth; if I prefer not Jerusalem above my chief joy (Ps. 137:1-6).

But even though they said they could not sing the songs of Zion in a strange land, *they ended up creating a song.* The song was different in harmony and in melody from the songs of the Babylonians. So we had a song different from the Indians, different from the whites, and different from the Africans back home. It was a unique song. It was the song of the oppressed. "I'm So Glad that Trouble Don't Last Always" wasn't an Indian song, nor a European song, nor was it an African song; it was God's song in our hearts in a strange land under the yoke of oppression.

There is a second difference. The practicing religion of the black church is a theology of survival, generally. It is also a carrier of the black folk culture. The practicing religion of the white church, with certain exceptions, has been American culture and racism. Ours is a theology of hope. I must underscore the fact that the black church is the carrier of black folk culture. Some people have almost forgotten that today. If you want true, authentic American black culture, you must go to the black church. With no offense intended, you can't find this in the Roman Catholic Church, or the Episcopal Church. How could a Mahalia Jackson have been born in a Catholic church? She would have to teach them that kind of music. How could a Martin Luther King, Jr., have been nurtured in the Church of England? It would be a contradiction of the church itself. The church would blow up in confusion. Can you imagine someone coming to Saint Paul's Cathedral and whooping like Ceasar Clark or a whole lot of us other black Baptists?

The black church has been distinguished greatly by a dynamic and free pulpit. The white church has had a circumscribed pulpit. The white pastor preaches, wondering if the trustees and deacons will approve. The black preacher is primarily concerned with whether God will approve.

Let me point out something else. When we didn't have any lawyers to interpret the meaning of constitutional rights, property rights, and human rights, the black pulpit was our defense. Even though the black preacher was not knowledgeable in the Justinian Code, the Code of Hammurabi, or the dynamics of Greco-Roman culture, even though he had not been to a law school, he did know "you've got to reap what you sow." When we didn't have any lawyers, the pulpit was our defense.

When we were torn apart all the week, for a few fleeting moments in that worship service we had an experience of togetherness. How were we torn apart? Somebody called us "boy," and we were over fifty, having lived a half century. Somebody called us "nigger," and that tore us apart. Somebody called us "darky," and that tore us apart. Somebody called us "granny," and we knew they were not our grandchildren. Somebody would call us "crazy." Someone would call us "mean, evil, and lowdown." Sometimes the children simply said "him," and the wife said "that one." But for a few fleeting moments in the "household of integrity," the black church, we got the notion that "I've got a new name over in Zion, and it's mine, it's mine, it's mine!" The black church has provided integrity.

The black church also provided social unity. It has provided a social house, a culture center, a freedom house. It has provided limited educational support. It has provided a meaningful spiritual legacy. The thrust for freedom by black Americans has found a home in the black church. Please remember that our mass meetings were not held in a cathedral or a synagogue. You remind some people of that. The operational base for Dr. Martin Luther King, Jr., was the black church.

Dr. Howard Thurman in *The Luminous Darkness* spoke eloquently concerning the black church and how it provides integrity and a sense of "somebodiness" to black people. He had this to say:

Black Church Distinctives 17

> It is a great irony that the Negro church has figured so largely as a rallying center for the civil rights movement in the South primarily because of its strategic position as an institution in Negro life; it has not become a civil rights rallying center because of its religious ethical teaching as such. But the logic of the impact of the religious experience in the Negro church made it inevitable that it would become such a center. For a long time the Negro church was the one place in the life of a people which was comparatively free from interference by the white community. A man may be buffeted about by his environment, or may be regarded as a nobody in the general community; a woman may be a nurse in a white family in which the three-year-old child in her care calls her by her first name, thus showing quite unconsciously the contempt in which she is held by his parents. When this Negro man and this Negro woman come to their church, however, for one terribly fulfilling moment they are somebody.[1]

The black church has converted oppression into poetry, exploitation into creative force, humiliation into a hunger for justice, haunting fears into hymns of faith. If this church is to remain relevant, it must convert a praying people into a positive power-conscious people. Prayer must find fulfillment in revolutionary action. Remember that prayer without action is empty. Remember also that action without prayer is dangerous.

The black church, then, was born in a political storm or a social storm, and I think it can do its best witnessing when the storm is raging.

Have you ever thought about the fact that without a psychiatrist, we withstood things that send most people to insane asylums? We didn't have the benefits of psychiatric counseling at the point of death, but the black preacher at the funeral service became the psychiatrist, without fee. The black church kept the black race from committing suicide. When we were living under the conditions of genocide (and we still are), the black church kept us alive on the inside, and we outlived, in many instances, the slave master; we took care of him and his children. At the same time, we survived with less than half enough.

We didn't need any dope. We didn't need any "speed." We didn't need any marijuana. You see, dope is the medicine of a slave. With all of the people talking about "revolution," you tell them that as long as they are on dope you will never have a spiritual revolution. Dope is designed to keep you enslaved. We have to say to the black community, "We need somebody to transport hope, because we already have too many importing dope." The black church ought to be, should be, the vehicle of hope in a hopeless world.

Some black people have gotten confused on this, and they are trying to make our churches European in style and content. Even many of our seminaries are sending out seminarians and seminary graduates trying to preach like other folk. "Stand right there and don't move." "Turn the page." "Quote a little verse and sit down." "When you can do that, we might invite you to give some remarks in our meetings sometimes."

Let me give you two examples of what I'm trying to suggest. Suppose Fred Shuttlesworth, Ralph Abernathy, and Martin Luther King, Jr., facing Bull Conner in Birmingham, had pulled out a prayer book, reading in Latin, and then called upon a European-styled choir director to lead the group in singing "A Mighty Fortress Is Our God." All of the waterhoses of Bull Conner would have washed the whole freedom movement down the very streets of history. The angels would have cried, and the devils would have giggled with glee.

Suppose somebody who has all of the fundamentals from the book in music is singing "Sometimes I Feel Like a Motherless Child." Let's say that the person has a degree in music, and that's wonderful. Let's say that they know all about A-sharp and A-flat, when to make a crescendo, and when to make a diminuendo; but one thing is lacking —they just can't sing. Some folks are trying to make us believe that our singing is uncultured; and because they can't sing, they elevate their nonsinging to the level of sophisticated culture and got us putting down our good singing for their nonsinging. Such a person would sing "Sometimes I Feel Like a Motherless Child" only with culture, but with no feeling.

On the other hand, take somebody else who knows what it means to walk to school with a lunch wrapped up in a little brown greasy bag; somebody who knows what it means to be required to move but nowhere to move; somebody who knows what it means to have to pay up but have nothing to pay down; somebody who knows what it means "to wet their pillows with the midnight dew (tears)," without any instruments but the music in their own souls. They can stand in the scorching heat of the noonday sun, bow their heads, and in the experience of their commitment cry out: "Sometimes I feel like a motherless child, a long ways from home."

Revolution starts in the heart after revelation. When the houses are burning down, revolution says we are looking "for a city which hath foundations, whose builder and maker is God" (Heb. 11:10). This ought to be the message of the black church in a confused world.

Note

1. Howard Thurman, *The Luminous Darkness* (New York: Harper and Row, 1965); quoted in *The Black Christian Experience,* Emmanuel McCall, comp. (Nashville: Broadman Press, 1972), p. 15.

2
Black Baptist Church History
Emmanuel L. McCall

When the first slaves arrived in America, in 1619, the idea prevailed that one *Christian* should not hold another *Christian* in bondage. This was an unwritten law. Among the theological debates of the 1600s and 1700s was the question of whether or not the slave had a soul. If it could be proven that slaves had souls, they could no longer be held in bondage. This issue was resolved by deciding that the slaves had a soul, but it was of a lower nature. "As one member of a much older slave society put it, some men were 'slaves by nature.' "[1] There was a long hesitancy among American churchmen to even attempt the evangelization of slaves and Indians. To do so was to acknowledge "the assumption of inner sameness of all men."[2]

"Many slaveholders felt that no matter how much conversion might benefit the Negroes' souls, it could only make them worse slaves."[3] They would thereafter press for freedom, status, and equality. History has proven that the most avid champions of human dignity have been converted slaves. Because of the fear of equality in heaven, "The Reverend Francis Le Jau reported from South Carolina that a lady had inquired of him, 'Is it possible that any of my slaves could go to Heaven and must I meet them there?' "[4]

Another excuse that was used to avoid the evangelizing of slaves was that they lacked the capacity to learn. Reverend Samuel Davies in a lecture to Virginia slaveowners corrected this misnomer when he said, "Your Negroes may be ignorant and stupid as to divine Things,

22 Black Church Life-Styles

... not for Want of Capacity, but for Want of Instruction; not through their Perverseness, but through your Negligence."[5] Cotton Mather echoed a similar theme in his *Small Offers towards the Tabernacle in the Wilderness* by saying, "They [the slaves] are kept only as *Horses* or *Oxen,* to do our Drugeries, but their *Souls,* which are as white and good as those of other Nations, their *Souls* are not look'd after, but are *Destroyed for lack* of *Knowledge.* This is a desperate Wickedness."[6]

This controversy lasted until 1667 when the Virginia legislature passed a law declaring "that baptism did not alter the condition of a person as to his bondage or freedom."[7] This act helped to remove the Christian religion as a legal barrier to slavery in the colonies.

The first Roman Catholic priests and missionaries in Maryland believed it their duty to enlighten slaves in church doctrine and other religious instructions. However, this policy was not generally true of Roman Catholic pioneers in this area.

The Protestant church had even a greater lag than that of the Roman Catholics in this area. The English seemed to be interested in finding new homes in America. They thought of blacks not as the objects of Christian love, but rather as tools with which they might achieve their goals. The English felt that the closer to servitude the slaves were kept, the more useful they would be as laborers; therefore, little concern was given for their spiritual needs.

England, desiring to maintain its hold on the colonies in America and to win more holdings in America from other nations, especially Spain and France, organized the Society for Promoting Christian Knowledge (SPCK) in 1699 and the Society for the Propagation of the Gospel in Foreign Parts (SPG) in 1701. The SPG gave much attention to evangelizing Indians and Blacks, both those who were free and those who were slaves. "The history of the S.P.G. and of its ally, the bishop of London, at times seems to consist largely of a series of hortatory sermons, instructions, pamphlets, reports, and letters of admonition."[8]

The geographical and communicative distance between England and America was one of those "mysterious ways in which God moved," for the religious leadership in England could not accept American attitudes towards slavery and used its influence for the good of the slaves. Winthrop Jordan suggested how difficult the communication was in his account of a Christian black named David.

David was given permission to preach by the Countess of Huntingdon, a Londoner who owned slaves in Georgia. James Habersham, a Savannah merchant, secretly slipped David out to England and sent this explanation of the near lynching David almost received:

> His Business was to preach a Spiritual Deliverance to these People, not a temporal one, but he is, if I am not mistaken, very proud, and very superficial, and conceited, and I must say it's a pity, that any of these People should ever put their Feet in England, where they get totally spoiled and ruined, [David had been to England] both in Body and Soul, through a mistaken kind of compassion because they are black, while many of our own colour and Fellow Subjects, are starving through want and Neglect. We know these People better than you do.[9]

Effects of the Great Awakening

The SPG was not to be credited with being the champion of slave freedom either by their influence upon the masters or the slaves. They did stir religious concern that paved the way for the religious experiences which came in the Great Awakening. The Great Awakening was the American version of the spiritual rebirth occurring in England in the early 1700s. This was prompted, not by a rebirth in theology, but by a rebirth and reformation of liturgy. A Congregationalist, Isaac Watts (known to most blacks as "Old Dr. Watts") developed a modern hymnody which allowed congregational participation. The more original versions—lined hymns—are still used in many black congregations but with the black charisma added.

The preaching of men like John and Charles Wesley was also part of the reformation of the liturgy. Worship came down from its high-church plateau and became the heartthrob of the common people. The worship of the middle and lower classes was greatly enhanced. The Wesleys exported their brand of religious expression to America and had an even more successful result. Along with such men as William Tennent, Sr., Gilbert Tennent, George Whitefield, Jonathan Edwards, and Samuel Davies, the Wesleys caused much spiritual stirring.

Their meetings were characterized by long, emotional sermons, shouting, fainting, leaping, laughing, jerking, rolling, barking, and many religious expressions previously unheard of and, in some quarters, unappreciated. The extreme between those desiring quiet formal worship and those caught up in the revival spirit led to divisions within denominations; the "Old Side" excluded the "New Side" among Presbyterians, the "Old Lights" excluded the "New Lights" among Congregationalists.

Especially in the frontier regions and South did this new religious expression gain strength. The camp meetings, brush-arbor meetings, and tent meetings were not only the scenes for religious expressions, but also the *sitz en leben* (situation in life) for the creativity of new religious expressions. For example, "spirituals," both black and white, had their birth out of the hardships and loneliness of both the frontier and slave situations. While there is a marked difference between these two types of spirituals, their rootage is similar.

Perhaps the most unnoticed result of the Great Awakening was the fact that the debate over whether or not blacks had souls ceased. Slaves were included in the camp meetings, brush-arbor meetings, and general evangelistic endeavors while attending the needs of their masters. Without seeking permission or further discussion, the slaves were experiencing the same emotional manifestations of their masters. Mass conversions occurred among the slave population. This prompted the need for continuing worship opportunities. Several developments can be noted:

1. On plantations where the owners were opposed to the Christian-

izing of slaves, religious exercise was prohibited. This led to secret meetings held in woods or other places of safety. Some features begun or developed out of those experiences continue even now, such as prayer circles, establishing tempo by the use of hands and feet, the singing of lined hymns, and the rise of charismatic preachers to guide the worship and to preach.

2. On plantations where the masters were Christian, or sympathetic to the evangelizing of slaves, several options developed. Some plantations had churches for the slaves. They were often presided over by a local white preacher. On occasions, a slave preacher would be allowed to "exercise his gift." He would be supervised by a white person to avoid the risk of having the slave preacher gain preeminence or preach insurrection. The slave preacher's role was often no more than that of an "exhorter." Often he only complimented the main sermon either by warming up the congregation or providing afterthoughts. In reality he was a translator of what the white preacher was trying to say.

The reasons some slave owners permitted the Christianizing of their slaves were mixed. Some were genuinely concerned about the total development of their slaves. Others, however, were moved by economic exploitability. Some missionaries advanced the notion that evangelizing the slave would make him a better slave rather than a worse one. He would be more docile, "tamed," less subject to rebellion than formerly so. One to advance such an idea was Dean George Berkeley who in 1725 tried

> to convince American planters "that it would be of Advantage to their Affairs, to have Slaves who should *obey in all Things their Masters according to the Flesh, not with Eye-service as Men-pleasers, but in Singleness of Heart as fearing God:* That Gospel Liberty consists with temporal Servitude; and that their Slaves would only become better Slaves by being Christians."[10]

A further statement was issued by the bishop of London in 1727.

26 Black Church Life-Styles

In a letter "To the Masters and Mistresses of Families in the English Plantations Abroad," he said:

> Christianity, and the embracing of the Gospel, does not make the least Alteration in Civil Property, or in any of the Duties which belong to Civil Relations; but in all these Respects, it continues Persons just in the same State as it found them. The Freedom which Christianity gives, is a Freedom from the Bondage of Sin and Satan, and from the Dominion of Men's Lusts and Passions and inordinate Desires; but as to their *outward* Condition, whatever that was before, whether bond or free, their being baptized, and becoming Christians, makes no manner of Change in it.... And so far is Christianity from discharging Men from the Duties of the Station and Condition in which it found them, that it lays them under stronger Obligations to perform those Duties with the greatest Diligence and Fidelity.[11]

Those slave owners who approved the Christianizing of their slaves out of economic expediency required a high morality content as well as an other-worldly emphasis. The slave was enjoined not to be wrathful or licentious; to keep the laws, obey the Sabbath, avoid drinking, and peace breaking; above all to be obedient. The end result was that he would go to heaven by being morally subservient. The inconsistency, of course, is that slavery created and nurtured the vices that the slaves were admonished to flee.

For example, how do you encourage a man to be faithful to his wife when you break up his family by selling his wife to one plantation and his children to another? The afflictions of the black family even now are the continuing impacts of the patterns set by the "Christian" forefathers since the 1620s. The source of this distorted view of morality is well expressed in Joseph Washington's observation:

> In 1726, the Evangelical Revival in Europe erupted in the Great Awakening in the colonies, The spirit was that of Calvinism. Calvinism has everywhere and always lacked interest in the common man, preferring

to oppose the sins of excessiveness and sensuality rather than those of inequality and injustice.[12]

3. Ample evidence abounds that many slaves were members of their masters' churches. Most often they could only participate in the worship, not in decision or other activities as equals. Often a "slave galley" or place at the back of the church or the side of the church was designated for them. There is an abundance of records indicating before and after the Civil War the desire for the separation of members based on racial identity. One example follows:

> The First Baptist Church, in the city of Louisville, Kentucky, was a white congregation, now known as the Walnut Street Baptist Church. This congregation had its beginning in the year 1815, just five years after Louisville became a city. As was the custom in most southern communities, Negro slaves were admitted as members, with very limited privileges and assigned seats in the balcony. In the year 1829, on the first Sunday in November eighteen slave members were given letters of dismission and were granted the privilege of worshipping to themselves, "under their own vine and fig tree."[13]

John Lee Eighmy says that:

> The desire for separation did not stop with the etiquette of distinction practiced when the races worshipped together. White Baptists made perfectly clear their preference for complete separation in religious life. State conventions often studied the problem of how best to give religious instruction to the colored. One theme runs through these reports: the method most highly recommended called for separate meetings and, whenever possible, the use of separate quarters.[14]

As unfortunate as this move was for the development of authentic Christianity in America, there was a side benefit for blacks. Apart from the folk religion that developed around the church, an authentic religious expression peculiar to blacks was free to fully express itself. Eventually there was the blending of that which was created when blacks worshiped in secret with that which was received from corporate worship with other Christians. The syncretism along with later developments gave form to the peculiarity of worship styles in black churches.

4. Another effect which the Great Awakening had was in the development of a social consciousness against slavery. Even as great reforms against coarse popular amusements, widespread illiteracy, injustice before the courts, child labor abuse, and industrial abuse followed the spiritual awakening in England, so did a consciousness for social justice develop in America. The religious climate in the North gave free blacks a platform for the attack on slavery. They were joined by some whites, especially Quakers, who extended their influence when possible into the South.

Noticeably absent was the prominence of a concerted abolitionist movement among white Baptists and Methodists in the South. This is of interest in light of the fact that most free blacks and slaves responded overwhelmingly to the Baptist and Methodist expressions of the Great Awakening. Because the economic support of those churches and their organizational structures depended on the slave owners, those churches and organizations were noticeably silent or negative on issues that would incite their constituencies. They retreated to a major emphasis of evangelism (soul saving) piety, moralism, otherworldliness. Their loyalty was clearly to "the Southern cause." Some even went so far as to sever ties with their northern counterparts, the Methodists in 1844, the Baptists in 1845.

The above is not intended to negate the influence of some voices among Baptists and Methodists in the South. Some did have pangs of conscience about the evils of the slave system. John Lee Eighmy cites the following as indications of concern among Baptists in the South:

> The earliest known Baptist action on slavery occurred in 1710, when a South Carolina church questioned the cruelty of punishments al-

lowed by the slave code. At the time of the American Revolution, many Baptists freed their slaves while churches vigorously entered into the antislavery debate. A Georgia association opposed future importation of slaves in 1793. Some Baptists in the Carolinas considered slavery to be incompatible with Christianity. . . . The General Committee, representing the state's six district bodies, condemned slavery as a "violent deprivation of the rights of nature" and then advised Baptists to "make use of every legal measure to extirpate the horrid evil from our land." Slavery became an even livelier issue farther west. Some pioneer preachers in Kentucky made opposition to slavery a matter of dogma. When the regular associational bodies would not adopt an antislavery position, emancipationists David Barrow, Carter Tarrant and others led 12 churches to organize a separate antislavery association.[15]

These voices for abolition were few and far between. For the most part Baptists and Methodists in the South were silent, neutral, or negative to such a "divisive" issue. Some churchmen of prominence such as Richard Furman and Richard Fuller even went so far as to prepare statements supporting slavery as necessary, divinely inspired, and biblically sanctioned.

In 1818, Presbyterians unanimously adopted a declaration citing slavery:

> A gross violation of the most precious of human nature, utterly inconsistent with the law of God, which requires us to love our neighbor as ourselves, and totally irreconcilable with the spirit and principles of Jesus Christ, which enjoin that "all things whatsoever ye would that men should do to you, do ye also to them."[16]

But the General Assembly still permitted slaveholders to hold office in the church, in spite of its statement concerning slavery as a gross violation of human rights. The violators were exhorted to "continue and increase their exertions to effect a total abolition of slavery, with no greater delay than a regard to the public welfare demands, and recommends that if a Christian professor shall sell a slave, who is also in communion with our church, without the consent of the slave, the seller should be suspended till he should repent and make reparations."[17]

Efforts to Help

In lieu of positive abolitionists activities, however, these denominations developed patterns of work intended to aid the religious development of black people. The history of Southern Baptists is illustrative.

After the Southern Baptist Convention was organized in 1845, one its first tasks was to plan for missionary work among black people. The Board of Domestic Missions (now the Home Mission Board) was "instructed to take all prudent measures for the religious instruction of our colored population." Southern Baptists continued this ministry by working with black Baptist churches, associations, and state conventions. They provided institutes, extension education centers, the American Baptist Seminary, teacher missionaries, regional missionaries, scholarship assistance, and financial support for agreed-upon projects. They supported salaries for blacks employed in denominational services of various kinds.

In the middle colonies the missionary work was led by Thomas Bray, who devised plans to convert adult blacks and to educate their children. It proved to be unsuccessful. Missionary work among blacks in Pennsylvania found less obstacles than in the other middle colonies. Blacks were baptized as early as 1712, shared in the worship, and attended services regularly. In the colonies farther north where fewer blacks were to be found, the problem of religious indoctrination was not too prevalent.

The "missionary movement" received another setback with the Puritans of New England. They desired to see blacks saved but did not want to see them connected with a state church that would give them political and religious freedom.

From 1750 to 1859 the controversy over slavery found its way into the churches. The reactions of the Southern religious bodies were decidedly proslavery. In many of the predominantly white churches, blacks voluntarily withdrew or were forced out. Whites also withdrew from churches which were predominantly black. However, in the latter's case they were not forced to leave by blacks but by social stigma. An excellent illustration is found in the origin of the Shiloh Baptist Church of Northumberland County, Virginia. In 1867, thirty-eight blacks, all members of the Fairfield Baptist Church (white) addressed the following letter to the white members:

> Poplar Stage,
> July 7, 1867

To Elder William Kirk and the Members of the
Fairfield Baptist Church

Beloved Brothers: Grace be unto you and peace from God, the father of our Lord Jesus Christ. From an earnest desire to act in all things with an eye single to the glory of God and for the unity of that common faith which constitute us in Christ Jesus, we have thought it advisable to counsel on the subject of our future church relation. So that whatever may be done we may at least preserve that peace and harmony which ought to characterize those of the same faith and order and promote the prosperity of that cause which, through your instrumentality, had been the means of calling us into the light and knowledge of the glorious gospel of the Son of God. Without alluding to the Providence that so mysteriously changed our social and political relation, we conceive that under the new order of things we are not only advanced in our religious privilege, but that solemn and weighty responsibilities impose upon us a new class of duties in which we should be wanting in fidelity if we did not seek to place ourselves in that position in which we could best promote our mutual good, both in reference to ourselves and our posterity. In this new relation the subject of a separate church organization presses itself upon us as the best possible way in which we can best promote those indispensable interests, such as an ordained ministry, a separate congregation with all the privileges of a church organization, stated church meetings, regular religious service, Sabbath schools, etc. But just at this point the question arises: Can we not do this and preserve the unity of the faith and continue in church fellowship with our white brethren; and thereby perpetuate our church identity, so that in all the general interest of the church we may be mutually interested and to some extent co-laborers? To effect this may require the concurrent action of all the members of the congregation concerned; and the object of this communication is to ask your attention to this subject with the hope that such an arrangement can be made as to induce a general church meeting at some convenient time and place for this purpose, that our identity may be preserved or perpetuated if possible; and if not, that we may receive your parting benediction and blessing, as well as your endonation [endorsement] of our Christian character and standing. All of which is most respectfully submitted for your prayerful consideration and action. Hoping that unerring wisdom may guide us in the way of all truth, we remain, dear brethren in the bonds of Christ.

>Yours Fraternally,
>Samuel Conway, Secretary
>Hirman Kenner, Chairman[18]

It is interesting to note that these people desired to carry out their wishes in the present church building, but on August 10, 1867, two white members donated small plots of land for a new church building. Whites continued to donate land and assist black Christians in establishing their own separate church houses.

The forced, voluntary, and/or intentional separation of black Christians gave rise to a new reality—black denominations. The intentional separation initiated by black people was necessary for them to determine their own destiny, by their own criteria, and with their own sense of personhood. For any cultural expression of faith to have validity and utility, the people must establish themselves in their own venacular. Black denominationalism was and continues to be movements in that direction.

Black Denominational Beginnings

Black churches and denominations developed from a three-pronged reality: (1) the earnest desire of every human to be in touch with divine realities, (2) the need for corporate expression of those realities in ways that honestly reflects a group's own experiences, (3) the past inability of white churches and denominations to relate to black experiences with integrity. These realities led black people to form their own resources and structures.

Black Christians are to be found in every major religious organization or denomination, even those that are predominantly white. Their numbers are not large in Episcopal, Lutheran, Catholic, Disciples, or Presbyterian denominations, nor is their presence distinctive in liturgical expression. In the late 1960s and 1970s, "black caucuses" developed as attempts to address the uniqueness of the black experience. At best they were sensitizers to predominantly white organizations and pressed for recognition in the body politic, but were short-lived. They were often separated from the main body of activity and primarily gave their leaders a platform. Black caucuses were eventually ignored while those few that remained within the main structure were given the recognition the caucuses tried to effect.

The denominations in which large numbers of blacks may be found are Baptists, Methodists, and a variety of Pentecostal churches. The Pentecostal and/or Holiness Church strength is due to the attractiveness of these churches in urban centers where they have provided free, creative, and emotional expression as compared to the sterility and sophistication of other churches. Yet the same churches that were once more sterile and sophisticated have embraced some features that distinguished Pentecostal and Holiness Churches, that is, use of tambourines, base guitars, drums, repetitive lines in music, or applause during sermons.

The large number of black people in Baptist and Methodist denominations is initially attributed to the pervasive influence of the Great Awakening revivalism.

Many blacks responded to Baptist expressions first because of the influence of their masters. Baptist polity did not require educational certification for membership. This not only suited the white frontiersman and Southerner, it was more attractive to the slave who was without educational opportunities. Secondly, there were no educational requirements for the ministry. A man could indicate his "sense of call," and if convincing enough before the congregation, he was sent forth to preach. This also appealed to the limited opportunities among slaves. Third, Baptists practice congregational autonomy. Anything that offered less outside interference and domination would have appealed to slaves. Finally, there was a mystical temperment to Baptist religious expressions. In baptism Baptists taught that God "troubled the waters." They were in tune with the mystery in the Lord's Supper. The special emphasis on kinship ("brother," "sister") linked the slaves close to their African heritage. This along with the easy appeal of emotional expression made Baptist religious affiliation accessible.

The Methodist attraction also came from the emphasis on radical conversion, emotional expression, enthusiastic preaching, but also an emphasis on structured organization. This appealed especially to the slaves desiring upward mobility and freedom from the lack of social and spiritual discipline.

While many blacks are in the predominantly white United Methodist Church, the majority are in the three black-controlled denominations—the African Methodist Episcopal Church (AME, 1816), the African Methodist Episcopal Zion Church (AMEZ, 1822) and the Christian Methodist Episcopal Church (CME). The CME was begun by white Methodists of the South in 1870 for blacks and until 1957 was known as the Colored Methodist Episcopal Church. In 1957, the CMEs changed "Colored" to "Christian."

One wanting an in-depth presentation on black Methodism would find such in Carol V. R. George's *Segregated Sabbaths,* (Oxford University Press, London: 1973), and Carter G. Woodson's *The History of the Negro Church.*

Black Baptist History

The first black Baptist church in America is reputed to be the church at Silver Bluff, South Carolina, organized between 1773-1775. Silver Bluff is across the Savannah river from Augusta, Georgia. The church was begun by a David George. George had been a slave of George Galphin who both permitted and supported religious inclinations. This congregation was driven into exile in 1778 when the British forced the evacuation of Americans in that area. In 1783, the Silver Bluff Church was revived under Jesse Peters.

In the 1778 evacuation, some slaves went over to the British in Savannah, Georgia, among whom was George Liele and some of the original members from Silver Bluff Church. Liele continued to minister to this group. He later baptized Andrew Bryan. Nine months after Liele's departure to Jamaica with his British master, a Colonel Kirkland, Bryan began preaching. He attracted a large following which was constituted into the First African Baptist Church, Savannah, Georgia, January 20, 1788. The church is referred to by some as the oldest black Baptist church with sustained existence.

This information conflicts with another presentation of data regarding black Baptist origins. In *Black Religion and Black Radicalism,* Gayraud Wilmore suggested that the first black church was formed by a white Separatist Baptist named Shubal Sterns on the William Byrd plantation in Virginia, 1758.[19] There are also claims made by churches in Williamsburg and Petersburg, Virginia, dating back to 1776. More data continues to be uncovered about the early history of black Baptist churches. The most definitive work is yet to be done.

As noted earlier, whites started a number of congregations for blacks in the early 1800s. Some even gave freedom to gifted slave preachers so that they could continue to preach. *Rhapsody in Black* is the story of John Jasper of Richmond, Virginia, who was clandestinely taught to read by his master's son. Later he was set free to preach and became one of the prominent preachers emerging from slavery. He was so forceful that his preaching won a large white following, thus intimidating the white clergy of Richmond.

While most blacks continued as members of their master's churches, the situation changed following the Civil War in 1865. The newly freed blacks wanted to express their freedom completely. They asked for letters of dismission from white churches and organized their own. The Fifth Street Baptist Church of Louisville, Kentucky, did this as early as 1835.[20] Some white churches forced the dismissal of black members.

After 1865 black Baptists formed their own associations, state, and regional conventions. These were formed primarily to assist the newly freed people in surviving. They provided money for educational opportunities, home economic training, trade and agricultural information, emergency sustenance, and all that a struggling people needed. The union of churches provided integrity (wholeness) without which the strivings of the race would have been impossible.

Efforts at Organization

One of the early black Baptist efforts at wider cooperation was the African Baptist Missionary Society (ABMS, 1815). From 1815-1845 this organization channeled its money for foreign missions through the American Baptist Union. In 1845 when Southern Baptists formed their own Convention, the ABMS channeled their resources through the SBC.

In 1821 the ABMS supported the missionary endeavors of Lott Carey and Collin Teague in Monrovia, Liberia. It also supported Solomon Cosby, W. W. Colley, and W. J. Davis.

There was an attempt to organize black Baptists on a larger scale. In 1840 the American Baptist Missionary Convention was organized for ministries in Northern and Midwestern states. The place of organization was the Abyssinian Baptist Church, New York City.

In 1864 the Western and Southern Missionary Baptist Convention was organized to meet the needs in states where the American Baptist Missionary Convention could not operate.

These two conventions merged in 1866 under the name The Consolidated American Baptist Missionary Convention (CABMC). They developed six district conventions of regional nature, but soon the development of district associations and state conventions overshadowed the CABMC, and it terminated in 1877.

In 1879 W. W. Colley returned from Africa, fired with zeal to promote foreign missions among black Baptists. Through personal appearances at local gatherings and by correspondence, he urged pastors to meet in Montgomery, Alabama, November 24-26, 1880. One-hundred-and-fifty-one messengers responded and organized the Baptist Foreign Mission Convention. W. W. Colley was elected corresponding secretary and officed in Richmond, Virginia. This organization while national in scope was committed only to foreign missions.

There was concern that mission interests should begin at home, for there were numerous needs of a people recently freed from bondage that had to be addressed. In 1886, William J. Simmons, president of State University (later named Simmons University) issued a call to which more than six-hundred messengers responded. On August 25, 1886 at Saint Louis, Missouri, the American National Baptist Convention was organized. Simmons was elected president. The singular purpose for this convention was to assist the spiritual and physical welfare of black people in America.

One of the ways of meeting these needs was through education. Many educational institutions developed. Some were begun by whites of the North, a few by whites of the South. Many were begun by the cooperative efforts of black Baptists who still desired to control their own destiny. While they were appreciative of any help offered, they were unanimous in their desire to be in control.

38 Black Church Life-Styles

The concern for resourcing black educational ventures led to the formation of yet another convention. In 1893 the National Baptist Educational Convention was organized. Now, black Baptists had three conventions, national in scope, but each singular in purpose. Since the resources for fulfilling these three objectives were coming from the same churches, the question of duplication of meetings loomed large in their concern. This led to a meeting to discuss possible consolidation in Montgomery, Alabama, in 1894. These three conventions agreed to suspend their annual meetings for 1895 and met in Atlanta, Georgia.

The National Baptist Convention, USA

On September 24, 1895, at the Friendship Baptist Church, Atlanta, Georgia, the National Baptist Convention USA was organized. This new convention resulted from the merger of the Baptist Foreign Mission Convention, the American National Baptist Convention, and the National Baptist Educational Convention. The organizations that birthed these conventions were structured in the new convention through boards: a foreign mission board, a home mission board, and an educational board.

Within two years, a serious conflict led to the formation of the Lott Carey Foreign Mission Convention. Rev. L. G. Jordan, corresponding secretary of the Foreign Mission Board, moved the offices from Richmond, Virginia, to Louisville, Kentucky. This action angered the east coast churches who had given heavily to foreign missions. There were also other regional concerns that highlighted the conflict: the desire of some to establish their own literature, a philosophical difference of conservatives vs. liberals, and a concern for whether or not foreign missions was being deemphasized. These concerns led to the establishment of a convention whose emphasis would be solely on foreign missions and named after the early pioneer Lott Carey who went to Africa from Norfolk, Virginia, in 1821.

It should be emphasized that to this day, the Lott Carey Foreign

Mission Convention is strictly a foreign mission convention. The churches affiliated with it, while belonging to other conventions, give generously to its foreign mission program. With executive offices in Washington, DC, the Lott Carey Convention sends at least 87 percent of its resources to actual mission work in the Caribbean, Africa, and India.

The National Baptist Convention USA experienced a second rupture on September 9, 1915, when controversy erupted over the ownership of the convention's publishing house in Nashville, Tennessee. Followers loyal to Dr. R. H. Boyd met at the Salem Baptist Church, Chicago, Illinois, September 9, 1915, and organized the National Baptist Convention of America (Unincorporated), sometimes called the "Boyd Convention." Until this time, the National Baptist Convention USA had not been incorporated. The Publishing Board had been incorporated under the laws of Tennessee and was not controlled by the convention. Following continued contests that spanned a nine-year period, the convention forces and those loyal to Dr. Boyd went in different directions. The National Baptist Convention USA did become incorporated and established a new publishing house controlled by the convention. It has since been named The National Baptist Convention USA, Inc. It has also been called by its strong leaders, the Townsend Convention, the Jackson Convention. (Both terms are now obsolete.) Both conventions have publishing houses in Nashville, Tennessee.

The National Baptist Convention USA, Inc., experienced yet further trauma in 1961 when a group concerned over tenure of office organized the Progressive National Baptist Convention, Inc. This followed a four-year struggle that began in the 1957 convention. Expecting that a four-year presidential tenure would be honored by president Joseph Harrison Jackson, some messengers came to Louisville, Kentucky, pledged to certain candidates. Through political processes, the convention rules were suspended and Dr. Jackson was reelected by acclamation.

Those disheartened by the action continued a struggle that lasted four years. Concluding that this was a no-win situation, L. Venchal Booth, pastor of the Zion Baptist Church, Cincinnati, Ohio, issued a call to those desiring an alternative convention style. At issue were not only the claims of oligarchical and presidential control, but questions about foreign missions and positive support of the civil rights movement led by Martin Luther King, Jr.

Booth's appeal got response from thirty-three messengers. The discussions resulted in many not wanting to form a new convention but to reform the NBC, Inc. A majority (by one vote) prevailed, however, and the National Progressive Baptist Convention, Inc., was born. This convention continues a strong emphasis on home and foreign missions, civil rights, and educational support. It has full-time executive staffs for its national office and its home and foreign mission organizations. It has been a consistent supporter of black colleges and theological institutions.

The National Baptist Convention, Inc., under the leadership of president Theodore J. Jemison of Baton Rouge, Louisiana, since 1982 has begun to recapture its former status as a supporter of black colleges, theological education, home missions, and issues of social justice. As an early pioneer in civil rights causes, Jemison set examples in Baton Rouge that were emulated by Martin Luther King, Jr. Even though the American climate has changed, Jemison has rekindled a social consciousness in black Baptists that has won admirers.

Other Black Baptists

While most black Baptists are in the National Baptist Convention, Inc., the National Baptist Convention of America, and the Progressive National Baptist Convention, they are also in other conventions such as the National Primitive Baptist Convention, the American Baptist Churches, and the Southern Baptist Convention. A significant number of churches do not belong to any organized body because (1) the churches are small; (2) many churches are rural; (3) most churches are pastored by bivocational ministers who have no time for denominational activities; (4) unless there are resources returned in services, denominational membership is meaningless.

There are over nine-hundred black churches in the American Baptist Convention denomination. Most of these are dually aligned with one of the National Baptist conventions.

The Southern Baptist Convention also reports black church membership in excess of eleven-hundred churches. Some of its churches are also dually aligned. The reason for dual alignment is for fellowship with the black community through the National Baptist Convention's activities, but to also take advantage of the program resources developed by the American and Southern Baptist structures. The later two have developed resources of personnel to service needs of the churches, publications, conferences, church loans, church pastoral assistance, and annuity programs.

Growth of blacks in the Southern Baptist Convention has been particularly interesting. Prior to 1861, black Baptists in the South belonged to the churches of their masters and were de facto Southern Baptists. After 1865 there were expulsions by whites of black members and the intentional departure of blacks from white churches. The trauma of the war and the new attempts at freedom by blacks did not allow extensive contact between white and black Baptists. The rise of "Jim Crow" laws and social restrictions further alienated them. Black Baptists went on to organize their own denominational structures to address their aspirations and needs.

It was not until 1951 that black churches were readmitted to the Southern Baptist Convention. The first was the Community Baptist Church of Santa Rosa California, followed by the Greater Friendship Baptist Church, Anchorage, Alaska. Additional churches were added in northeastern, western, and north central states. In the late 1960s and early 1970s black Southern Baptist churches were developed and/or accepted in the Deep-South states. As of 1983 all states where

Southern Baptists had state conventions had black churches in their memberships.

The new phenomena of the 1970s was the aggressive effort by Southern Baptists to start churches in black communities. This was spurred by (1) the open acceptance of blacks in the SBC, (2) the inability of whites to attract blacks to their churches, (3) the desire to retain congregations that might be lost in transitional communities, (4) and the commitment to Bold Mission Thrust (BMT). BMT is a planned coordination of each SBC agency and denominational unit to see to it that every person in the United States has a chance to hear the gospel proclaimed and become a member of a New Testament church fellowship by AD 2000. With the planned emphasis on evangelism and new church starts, the number of black Southern Baptists will easily triple by AD 2000.

The irony of the Southern Baptist Convention is that it once was the most reactionary as far as creative race relations were concerned.

And What of the Future?

In lectures and classes on black Baptist history, the question is often asked if the three national bodies will ever merge. While that is left for the future to disclose, it is encouraging to see the gestures of fellowship and cooperation that continue to be rekindled. The current leaders wisely emphasize the futility of "eating the sour grapes planted by the fathers." They continue to encourage their constituencies to pull together for the good of the race. Whether or not they merge organizationally is not as important as their willingness to cooperate on vital issues. Those issues include the support of historically black colleges and seminaries, justice in America and abroad, the strengthening of clergy, of churches, of church resources, and addressing all issues that affect the health of America and the wholeness of black people.

The predominantly white Southern Baptist Convention churches will continue to start new congregations in black communities. Their efforts should not be viewed as a threat. They have no desire to "take over" black denominations or institutions. With pain for the past, they seek to be the Christians they should have been. There continues to be room for cooperative endeavor between the SBC and the three National Baptist Conventions. The strategies and structures for that cooperative endeavor may need to be redefined. Remodeling outmoded structues is insufficient for the tasks to be completed.

As one who has spent the last eighteen years in trying to help black and white Baptists in cooperative ministries, this writer is optimistic about the potentials for the future. God keeps doing the unexpected among His people. With tiptoed expectancy, we watch to see what He will do next and to join Him in the venture.

Notes

1. Winthrop D. Jordan, *White Over Black* (New York: W. W. Norton & Co., Inc., 1968), p. 179.
2. Ibid., p. 180.
3. Ibid., p. 181.
4. Ibid., p. 183.
5. Ibid., p. 188.
6. Ibid., p. 190.
7. Harry V. Richardson, *Dark Glory* (New York: Friendship Press, 1947), p. 1.
8. Jordan, *White Over Black*, p. 208.
9. Ibid., p. 210.
10. Ibid., p. 191.
11. Ibid., p. 191.
12. Joseph R. Washington, Jr., *Black Religion* (Boston: Beacon Press, 1964), p. 182.
13. Emmanuel L. McCall, *Centennial Volume* (Louisville: Standard Printing Company, 1968), p. 148.
14. John Lee Eighmy, "The Baptists and Slavery: An Examination of the Origins and Benefits of Segregation," *Social Science Quarterly*, #49, No. 3, Dec. 1968, pp. 666-673.
15. Ibid., pp. 66-667.
16. Leonard H. Haynes, Jr., *The Negro Community Within American Protestantism*, p. 65.
17. Ibid., p. 114.

18. Richardson, *Dark Glory,* pp. 14-15.
19. Gayraud Wilmore, *Black Religion and Black Radicalism* (Maryknoll, N.Y.: Orbis Books, n.d.), p. 79.
20. McCall, *Centennial,* p. 148.

3
Black Nurture
Ella Mitchell

When I was a child in South Carolina, our household included two grandmothers who had been born in slavery and were barely literate. But they were capable of magnificent comments on the Bible, and they could quote it seemingly for days. I was long since into my middle years when the full significance of this achievement finally struck me. Neither grandma had had the benefit of printed curriculum or trained church school teachers. There were no Sunday Schools at all in their early years. Yet, without a doubt, the truths of the gospel were in their very bones. What manner of training could have been so amazingly effective?

It can now be declared with confidence that the answer was, and is, a rich black tradition, formal and informal, of what may be called Christian education, church education, or educational ministries. The fact that the black experience is still so different from America's majority experience has finally helped many to see why a different "culture kit" for coping is so natural, even mandatory. Now, since learning is always done in a cultural context, it should be easy to see why, without conscious intent to vary from dominant patterns, my grandmas' parents taught them differently. The fact that my great-grandparents were completely illiterate or preliterate is beside the point. Their educational results speak for the unquestionable existence of a pattern of pedagogy of impressive, if not outright awesome, effectiveness.

To understand this early teaching more fully, it appears wise to examine its earliest development. This requires a kind of "roots" inquiry or tour all the way back to West Africa. You see, most of the oral communication and instructional patterns used are traceable, not to American missionaries, but to the independent, African-based culture of the slave quarter and its underground church, or the "invisible institution." The stream of culture which preserved the African patterns was, in other words, wholly independent, separate, and distinct from the spasmodic missionary efforts. This otherwise unlikely separateness can be charged in part to the very missionaries who sought to suppress African culture as heathen. Little did they know how close African traditional religion was to the early Old Testament, or how powerful the African teaching methods were.

I cannot honestly claim that I set out intentionally to find out how my grandparents learned so much so well. If I had been trying, I don't believe I would have had any idea where to look. Then the whole thing leaped out at me one day in Ibadan, Nigeria. There I saw not grandmas but young children capable of quoting at length from their culture's collection of proverbial wisdom. They could even provide interpretation. Yet, when we asked when and where they had gained this phenomenal knowledge, they were tongue-tied. They seemed not to have any term for formal teaching-learning, and thought they had "always known" these things. It dawned on me that this was the best possible way to learn values and beliefs, and this must have been the same way my grandparents were taught, whatever the method.

Of course, the expertise of these children was far from accidentally communicated. Their culture assumed that this wisdom was a corpus come from God. No child was equipped for life without such knowledge. Their culture provided innumerable opportunities to convey this crucial insight for life, and every responsible parent found it relatively easy to make certain that the child was fully trained, or in a sense "indoctrinated."

This traditional African concern about training is illustrated by an experience we had with a student removed from his native land. He waxed rather eloquent when he spoke of his wife who was soon to join him in this country. Naturally, we all assumed that she would fit the American prototype of attractive womanhood. To our surprise, the African lady who arrived was very plain in appearance and roughly half again as large as her husband. Our careful listening to his comments, however, revealed that a totally different set of criteria for wives existed in his culture. This student was ecstatic over his wife's profound grasp of African traditions and value systems. As a member of a highly child-oriented society, he looked for a bottom line of well-reared children, utterly oblivious to such shallow concerns as feminine pulchritude. This African student's high expectations may have been too much for an ordinary parent to achieve on American soil. But the very structures and communal life of African society made child rearing relatively easy. Our student's dream of effective parenthood was quite workable on his home turf.

From the outside, the view of modern African society is misleading at this point. The subtleties of relationship and world view have been much less vulnerable to the pressures of modernity than appears on the surface. John S. Mbiti has suggested that even when people were converted to Christianity or Islam ("contact" religions), they maintained the "instant" religion of the original culture.[1] Looking from within today's African traditional culture, one can discern with accuracy the broad outline of world view and teaching methods which were brought to these shores two and three centuries ago. Obviously, such things as the suppression of drumming and the pressures of the typical work day required our ancestors to engage in cultural adaptations. But the basic character of belief and its transmittal was tenaciously maintained from Africa to America and on through succeeding generations.

The African society used and uses a wide variety of cultural vehicles in the instructional task. Storytelling was an extremely lively and popular artform used in teaching. Audiences, both formal and infor-

48 Black Church Life-Styles

mal, were willing to listen seemingly for days on end. The memories of these fascinating storytellers were like those of the griots in Alex Haley's *Roots* saga. Yet lessons of sorts were being beamed constantly to children as adults celebrated life's occasions or just gathered impromptu. Stories entertained or served to settle weighty matters. Everybody knew how the plot would come out, but they enjoyed reliving the experience and treasured the unique artistry of each raconteur.[2] Further interest was generated by the large amount of audience participation expected from young and old alike. It would be hard *not* to learn the values of the society in such a communicative context, enlivened by the mixing in of poetry and music, and even dance and drumming. Yet typical adults, like the boys in Ibadan, would hardly know what was meant above by "art form used in teaching."

One is tempted to speak of each art form separately, but stories were often used as settings for songs, explaining and giving them meaning. At any point, the variety might be enlarged to include proverbs, dancing, and drumming.[3] Interaction with the performers was and is desirable, and by comparison with Western-style performance, the whole experience would seem to be characterized by great enjoyment and expression of feeling. Nevertheless, the informal renditions might serve any number of very utilitarian purposes, such as a dispute to be settled, a bargain to be driven, a child to be corrected, or a friend to be advised of the error of his or her ways.[4] It goes without saying that work was made easier by singing, fields were thus converted into classrooms with "live entertainment."

Proverbs are hardly thought of as art, yet they were often expressed with poetic beauty and were ubiquitous in palavers and spontaneous discussions. Black Africans were and still are expected to ride the horse of proverbs to get most swiftly to the ideas sought.[5] These pearls of wisdom were the basis for survival and cohesion in the extended-family/tribal unit. A proverb about this genre states: "An elder with a poor memory whose old people told him nothing is a very small boy among the elders, and might well be looked upon with contempt by younger persons" (Yoruba).

With such importance given to proverbs, it is easier to understand why the boys in the streets of Ibadan knew them.

While there, we attended a festival for the "living dead," a common aspect of African culture. Small children in traditional costumes took a major part in the pageantry, turning no-hand back flips and executing intricate dances. I thought it especially "nice" that this festival should recognize small children and give them such a prominent place on the program. What I realized later was that this was done with several purposes in mind, not the least of which was the fact that all these flips and pantomimes were teaching the tradition of the society. They were having fun and being recognized, but that was why they were learning so well.

Clearly the children we had met were not geniuses; they were run-of-the-mill products of an ingenious educational system. There was no escaping the teaching of their ancestors, dead or living. The living spent much time communicating with them, and the living dead were brought to mind and sight by the celebrations in which they had so large a part. They were *surrounded* by the lesson, and this was so natural they didn't recognize it as instruction.

The place and dazzling effectiveness of memory in the oral traditions of Africa deserve special treatment. However, cold terms like "accuracy" and "effectiveness" are loaded with inappropriate Western connotations of overdependence on words as such. The phrase "faithful transmittal" comes a bit closer to the real meaning. The idea is that succeeding African generations gained a total involvement in the tradition, avoiding the erosion of faith/culture suffered by such groups as the Puritans in New England. Traditional African religions needed no "halfway covenant," such as the Puritans had to try to keep the succeeding generations within the community of faith, despite an unacceptable level of commitment to the common heritage. Even now, the African tradition is alive and surprisingly well in much of

West Africa, notwithstanding the assaults of trade, industry, and urbanization on the traditional society.

It would also be true that Christianity and Islam have caused far fewer significant changes in the basic culture than is commonly assumed. In fact, Christians and Muslims are still culturally African, showing "instant" traditional African responses to life's major crises. Even the typical professional African will return to traditional rituals and remedies in illness and go back to the village for the festivals. I was once involved in a daylong set of both Anglican and traditional African ceremonies for the naming or christening of a West African friend's baby, eight days after birth. Weddings among such trained families are known often to take a week, to get in all Christian and traditional African rituals. This traditional culture and religion were no less tenacious when they faced Christianity on American soil.

The impressive memory capacity is manifest in the huge volume of oral literature preserved in Africa today. The processes of African oral teaching have even been tested and found to be equally as effective as teaching methods using books. Added to this is the fact that the oral use of songs and so forth has been far more pleasant, attracting visitors and increasing motivation. The oral process, in other words, is a legitimate system of teaching and learning, not just a naive pattern that happens to have good memory as a by-product.

Perhaps the most awesome of all memory exercises is the body of materials an Ife diviner has to learn. In order to guide his counseling and healing of clients, he has to know the sixteen odus which go with the sixteen squares on a divining board, or 256 odus. A minimum of four stories goes with each of these odus, for a starting repertoire of 1024, but experienced diviners know sixteen for each or some 4,096 tales.[6] Memory is obviously a highly developed skill among Yoruba religious professionals, but the tendency prevails throughout this culture and virtually all other cultures of West Africa.[7]

When one observes the Ibadan children learning so accurately the wisdom of their ancestors, one is watching in practice the same general process used by blacks in slavery. It was applied to the Bible, which was adopted as a local replacement for their previous sacred wisdom.[8] No wonder my preliterate great grandparents knew it so well! It was by just such intergenerational teaching or oral tradition that the preliterate versions of the early Bible manuscripts were originally kept intact. They were finally written down in what we refer to as the books of the Old and New Testaments. (It is comforting to me to know that beloved ancestors used some of this method among us as recently as the early 1920s.)

Only recently have we come to see that African traditional religious instruction is the precise starting place of black-on-black instruction in this country. A stream of literature has been written, starting in 1958 with Herskovitz, to correct the error of earlier scholars who thought blacks were stripped of their African culture. The process of catching, shipping, "seasoning," and selling slaves did not in fact denude the Africans of their cultural techniques for coping. Hard evidence is so very easy to spot that one wonders how African cultural survivals were overlooked for so long. African drum telegraphy, with all its complicated code, had to be *outlawed* in this country! This skill was that well preserved after the Atlantic crossing!

African homeopathic medicine had to be prohibited (for use among whites) because it had been so fully accepted in this country. Likewise, traditional African religious gatherings were forbidden—and so went into underground observances—that varied greatly from the worship which was practiced in the churches officially permitted and supervised among slaves.

So it should not be the least surprising that it was especially hard to squelch the way slaves had of teaching their children. Parents had to work from "kin to cain't" (from sunup to sundown), but elderly grandparents were expected to care for and teach the small children. Until they were large enough to work, there was plenty of time to listen to tales and take advantage of the peak learning years. Days were long and hard, equal to available sunlight for work. But the elderly were expected to do the typical African honors with the small children. When the children were old enough to go to the fields, the singing and palaver of the African type were still in place in one form or another. Furthermore, there was no effort to control what went on in cabins in the oft-too-short hours from sundown to sunup. The results speak for themselves. Thousands of slave narratives attest to the fact that slave children were exceptionally well trained in devious ways for coping with the masters, *and* in Bible wisdom, prayer, and trust.

It is commonly assumed that there was much missionary work done among the slaves, so the typical reader will immediately wonder why so much of religious training is credited to the initiative of the slaves themselves. The answer is that *history clearly shows no major missionary effort among the slaves, in America, ever.* Early slaves were often considered not to have souls capable of being saved. Missionary efforts even among whites were few and far between prior to the revolutionary war. The single exception was the first Great Awakening, which was not known for emphasis on instruction as such. Just about the time there seemed to be some serious interest in reaching and teaching the slaves for Christ, the most threatening of the slave rebellions broke loose. The insurrections of 1821 (Denmark Vesey in South Carolina) and 1831 (Nat Turner in Virginia) destroyed virtually all enthusiasm for learning among the slaves. It was feared that Jesus would be properly understood and rebellion encouraged. This took all the steam out of a never-really-robust missionary movement, leaving only fragmentary effort.

In the two-hundred years prior to this time, slaves gained their profound understanding of Moses, the Emancipation, and so forth from sources surely other than masters. Of course, the Church of England did send a tiny few missionaries after it was decided that blacks did have souls (1666). But that august body did not have enough priests to begin to reach its original constituencies in Virginia and points south, much less the Indians and Blacks. Furthermore, the

Black Nurture 53

poor quality of most of those priests and the hardships of frontier life and travel left even the whites in a lamentable state of faith. With reading by blacks soon outlawed and with white religion at a very low ebb prior to the two Great Awakenings, blacks went it on their own. They prayed, sang, and taught in underground gatherings, in family cabins, in the extended-family society of the slave quarter, as well as in the fields where they worked.

Wherever blacks were involved with white-sponsored religious teaching, the limits were great. White preachers had little to say save Paul's opener about slaves obeying your masters. They "forgot" to quote his punch line about there being only *one* master: God (Eph. 6:9). They also overdosed them on "Thou shalt not steal" (Matt. 19:18). But slaves knew the gospel message meant far more than this, and they often voted against it with their feet—walking out. When their own preachers were permitted to hold services, a white monitor was legally mandated. And this, too, put a damper on relevant biblical preaching and teaching. Thus, the unmistakable fact is that the phenomenon of profoundly black Christianity in the nineteenth century was surely the result of their own initiative, creativity, and adaptability, operating on an African culture base plus their own awesomely correct biblical interpretations.

How, then, can one describe the slave adaptations of the African childrearing which made of my preliterate ex-slave grandmothers such warm, rich interpreters of the Word? The question takes on major significance because these women were not unusual. Indeed, the same world view and value system by which they maintained sanity and creativity sustained virtually all slaves in the horror chamber of bondage.

The first aspect of the slave style of rearing children was closely shared living or what has been referred to as "enforced intimacy." It was parallel in intensity to the intimacy of the small African family/ village. Working belief systems for addressing the issues of life were more caught than formally taught. Thus, slave children got their cues for coping by watching their parents and other significant adults at very close range. They were together in cotton and cornfields, in small cabins, and in the highly restricted life of the slave quarter. Persons were so close that, blood relations or not, one had to treat all as persons and indeed as kin. Training for coping with tragic mistreatment was thus handed down most effectively with no formal instruction but with lots of casual oral communication.

A classic example is seen in the courage of the little slave Charlotte, age eight, who saw her beloved mother, Fannie, cruelly beaten and sent away.[9] The helplessness and sense of outrage could have been so traumatic as to scar her very soul for life. Yet she reported accepting her mother's stern instructions during the departure, and she carried them out with calm resolve. The clue to this remarkably mature behavior lies in the fact that the mother endured it all with faith and unflinching personal dignity. The child knew no better than to assume that this was the way life had to be, and her heroic conduct was partly due to having seen no other example from which to choose. Her repertoire of responses was on a high level but limited to what had been gained in an intimate circle of loving adults.

A crucial facet of belief, hard to teach, yet learned in intimacy, was self-esteem. In fact, the lesson was learned so well that despite the ravages of dehumanization, very few slaves ever gave up and fully accepted the servile image thrust upon them. One antidote for the perpetual put-down was the love lavished on babies in the slave quarter. Save among the elderly, there was little time to spend with them. But the entire quarter blazed with a love and acceptance that never died in the depths of those born in bondage. It was traceable to the adoration—almost worship—poured out on babies in the prior African culture.

Historian John W. Blassingame says:

> Since slave parents were primarily responsible for training their children, they could cushion the shock of bondage for them, help them to

understand their situation, teach them values different from those their masters tried to instill in them, and give them a referent for self-esteem other than their master.[10]

Nuclear family love was paralleled by an emphasis on friendship and love throughout the slave community which greatly influenced learning. Bereft of other treasures, one treasured relationships. The love and care lavished on infants did not die at the walking stage or the talking stage, or even at puberty. The whole quarter was a collection of extended family kin who loved the young and accepted responsibility for them. (The pattern has not died. There are blacks of recent generations who can testify to having been the beneficiary of spanking by any mother on the block, or even in the neighborhood.) The other side of that coin is that children were loved and *taught* by that same impressive cadre of neighbor/relatives. What these surrogate parents taught was penetrating, because their love made of them significant personages or influences. The classic way in which they bore the burden of slavery was in part based on a belief system learned/taught by contagion.

Of course, the message of self-respect and psychic survival could not be trumpeted openly. Therefore, the caught-not-taught process was especially convenient in the quarters. Casual conversation and example could quietly nourish healthy self-awareness in the hearts of even the youngest children.

"My Pa had Bible tales he never told the White chillun."[11] What she meant was that her father was a regular "Uncle Remus" and talented as an extremely entertaining raconteur, but he was well aware of the power of an oral tradition to nourish identity and determination. He could give the interpretation and meaning to life on which all these other spiritual factors had to be based.

Again, this enforced intimacy of living, seasoned with love, was all the more influential in rearing slave children because of the added importance of communication and expression. With limited living

56 Black Church Life-Styles

space and no outside contact or material resources, slaves learned the value of expressing themselves just to affirm their personal being and power to act. Western culture is familiar with Descartes's *"cogito, ergo sum,"* "I think, therefore I am." Likewise, the slaves might have said, "I speak, therefore I am." It was a way of clinging to a spark of vibrancy in a life otherwise often unpleasant.

Intensive verbal communication was crucial to psychic survival and sanity, but it also added to the likelihood of a child's gaining some casual but crucial value judgment or witness of trust. The influence was often increased because the lesson was eagerly overheard rather than urged on unwilling ears. Children hung on every word of adult exchange in a slave quarter where conversation was so important. And children were taught to speak and share with each other and with God, in prayer. An interesting example is found in the literature of slave narratives or autobiographies:

> I can remember how my mother used to pray out in the field. We'd be pickin' cotton. She would go off out there in the ditch a little ways. It wouldn't be far, and I would listen to her. She would say to me: "Pray son," and I would say, "Mother, I don't know how to pray," and she would say, "Well just say, Lord, have mercy." That gave me religious inclinations. I cultivated religion from that time on. I would pray and finally I learned. One day I was out in the field and it was pouring down rain, and I was standing up with tears in my eyes trying to pray as she taught me to do.[12]

The rapport between children, parents, and other adults was heightened further by the urgency of the situation. Children learned early of death and danger. The gravity of their plight was obvious, and slave parents dared not try to protect their offspring from hard reality. The best evidence of this fact is the sophistication among small children in dealing with situations where survival was at stake. The stereotype of slave children as happy and innocent animals is wide of the mark. The following example cinches the case:

I was a little gal, but I remember how the white folks would come by, way back yonder in the old days, and ask me where was the niggers, and I would tell them, "I don't know." They would keep after me and sometimes I would tell them that they had went away and that was all that I knowed. They used to tell me if I would tell them what they wanted to know that they would give me some candy. Of course I, like other children, liked candy very much, but never could hardly get it. They would give me the candy but I would only tell them that they went away, and I didn't know where they went, just went away. Sometimes they'd ask me, "Where is your mammy, little nigger?" and "Ain't you got no mammy?" and "If you will tell me, I will give you some candy." I used to say sometimes, "Will you, sure 'nough?" and they would say, "Yes." They would give me the candy and I would tell them she had gone to keep the Yankees from getting her.[13]

At another point, this same little girl had seen her mother beaten every morning for days. With her mother in danger of being whipped to death, this child did not have to be convinced of the importance of her mother's warnings. Her intense attention was guaranteed in order to survive in a circumstance tantamount to wartime siege. In fact, no child aware of the constant threats would dare take lightly the words of any responsible slave adult.

A happier aspect of slave rearing was the more typical formal religious instruction. While learning to read the Bible was outlawed, a few "kind" and daring owners and others taught blacks to read anyhow. However, with or without reading, Bible teaching was the closest thing they could get to formal training. Such learning as this was viewed not only as spiritual food but as a means of improving their condition. All learning was thought of as skills keys to abundant living, and the hunger for instruction defies description. As soon as the Civil War was over, the learning explosion was phenomenal because of the thirst for knowledge engendered during slavery.

For instance, Elijah John Fisher (1858-1915), later pastor of the famous Olivet Baptist Church of Chicago, completed a college degree in record time even though his degree included the biblical languages. When he entered Atlanta Baptist Seminary (Morehouse College), after substantial qualifying reading, he was placed in the senior class. This was his only year of formal training. Prior to this he had a month under an ex-house slave and ten more months under a white missionary. He overcame a tremendous physical handicap to become an intellectual and spiritual giant in the black church of his time.

The final facet of child rearing among slaves is a composite of almost all that has preceded; it is called "oral tradition." In a sense, the purposeful singing, drumming, dancing, and narration of African culture never ceased. The grim details of slave life listed above never succeeded in dampening the irrepressible spirits of black children, which may explain why they were perceived by slaveholders as enjoying their plight. This ironical combination of opposites is perhaps better envisioned in a sample of the oral tradition itself: a tale used to teach slave children how to cope. It was about Brer Rabbit, a powerless rabbit playing for his life. Yet the tale was hilarious, as were the fascinated and forewarned children who heard it. Uncle Remus as prototype of the elderly raconteur is a well-established personage in American folklore. But much more importantly, he represents a very powerful, subtle tradition of conversation/communication growing out of African tradition. It was preserved because it was so crucially useful, and it differed from the African original only in that it occurred among far fewer festive occasions. The oral tradition prepared children for a far harder life in America, but it performed the task amazingly well.

Oral tradition performed the same function after the slaves were freed, with only two changes: the restrictions on movement were reduced, diminishing somewhat the level of enforced intimacy in the extended family; and there was a massive new emphasis on formal education, reading, writing, and arithmetic. However, this latter did not take the place of oral tradition in the deeper matters of how to cope in oppression and the development of an adequate belief system.

In fact, formal education itself was often fused or blended with oral traditional forms of instruction in many creative ways.

As recently as the early 1920s I was happily involved in this very kind of mixed methods of instruction. It carried over into spontaneous play among us children, aged five to eleven. The setting was a plank stretched between two supports on which children bounced. It was a seesaw in reverse, in that the ends were fixed and the middle went up and down. We called it a "juggling board." Under the leadership of the eleven-year-old we bounced to a distinct rhythm, all the while counting or singing out the letters of the alphabet or naming the states of the Union. The same singsong homework accompanied our rope skipping away from school, and it mattered not that no adults were there to prod or approve.

This cultural momentum applied to our studies under teachers as well. At "Missy Sanders's School" in Charleston, South Carolina, the teacher marched her second- and third-graders on the "Bah'try" singsonging not only the states but their capitals. This phase of learning was by rote, but it was fun, and I haven't seen a more effective method of memorization since.

The character of the African/slave teaching pattern continued in still another way: the white missionary schoolteachers who swarmed southward to teach empowering skills were not removed from intimate contact with their pupils and their families. Misunderstood and hated by Southern whites, these Northerners were pressed into the warm and intimate life of the black community. Their informal witness thus reinforced their formal instruction and, in addition, illustrated in real life the faith and ethics taught in the classroom. The "black Puritans" of today's Southern black middle class are strong testimony to the effectiveness of the values lived out by New England schoolmarms in the black ghettoes of the South a century ago.

It turns out that this education was a mixed blessing, since the teachers provided partially alien models, and since they were paternalistic, but they were also *parental.* As such, many were almost never off the job, eating their meals in the same hall with their boarding students. It was theirs also to distribute the "barrels" of clothing sent to the almost-always-needy students. For students accustomed to an intimate family structure, they served literally *in loco parentis,* caring deeply, and unaware of the subtle ways in which they were teaching students to wish that they were white also.

As time went on, there were more and more black teachers, and the close ties prevailed among them too. "Cousin" Missy Sanders's school was in her home as were many family-operated and community-operated schools. One went to her house as one went to Grandma's or Aunty's. Thus, when I as a kindergartner was pushed into a large mud puddle, Cousin Missy thought nothing of taking me upstairs, cleaning me up, and dressing me for the day. It became an honor to wear the teacher's blouse as a dress, and her warm, unceremonious devotion to my needs taught a great lesson in crucial self-esteem.

Alongside the day schools for readin', writin', and 'rithmetic were the Sunday Schools, held in homes as well as churches. They were often held wherever the day school was held, and they were the pride and joy of both black church and community. This went on from the close of the Civil War until well into the twentieth century. But these classes were designed to follow white church program models and to provide a more "proper" religious instruction than had been provided, presumably, by the oral tradition.

It is interesting to note that the very first Sunday Schools in America were organized (as early as 1785-87) with poor freedmen and slaves in mind. While the Sunday Schools reaching blacks in the North were few in number, and those in the South were fewer still, this instrument of instruction was to become a firm and fixed part of the American dream of nurture in the mind of almost every slave. The fact that the first white Methodist to teach blacks in Sunday School was punished for doing it only added to the tenacity with which the dream was held.

Following the Civil War, this dream was aided and abetted by hundreds of Sunday School missionaries and colporteurs, black and white, who busily organized Sunday Schools with or without churches to match or sponsor them. This corps of workers served in addition to the missionary day-school teachers, and many new missions and full-blown churches grew out of their burgeoning Sunday School movement. There were Sunday Schools in many places where they couldn't manage day schools, and they involved a far wider circle of black laity.

Therefore, training teachers for biblical instruction became an important task, and most Northern denominations joined in the fruitful mission. Quite often this effort was aided and coordinated by the powerful International Sunday School Association. When black and white joint sponsorships of the missionaries dwindled, the emphasis shifted to training the teacher candidates at the church-sponsored colleges. It was assumed that whole student bodies would soon go forth trained in and committed to Sunday School teaching.[14] The impact of this change of strategy was to be seen on black Christian college campuses as recently as the 1960s with "model Sunday Schools" preceding Sunday morning chapel. However, the results back at the local churches from which the students came were far short of the game plan. The efforts were heroic, but the approach was culturally naive. College students who had been taught to spurn indigenous folkways were ill prepared to work effectively in the churches of the black masses. Thus they were seen as "uppity," and the home church leaders retained control of their only arena for the exercise of leadership. So the Sunday Schools continued without major influence from Northern denominational and interdenominational agencies, save in the provision of literature.

Even that changed radically early in the twentieth century. Whole denominations voted to sponsor and control the writing, editing, and publication of their own educational materials. However, while this was a major step, it was not until the 1960s that the literature produced began to reflect heightened concerns for uniquely black needs.

Thus the cultural and structural patterns of the earlier Sunday School prevailed despite black control.

Of course, there emerged some black churches of middle-class culture, and in these usually urban congregations, college graduates were invited and even urged to teach. The numbers were smaller and the spirit not nearly so high, but the general tendency was for the educated to opt for upward mobility. The struggle of returning to the churches of their childhoods was too great. In addition, it seemed too much like slipping "back into ignorance." Black graduates who were healthily bicultural were very rare, and they who were willing to "risk such loss of status" were a welcome breed indeed among the black masses.

This absence of professionals seemed not in the least to dampen the ardor of the uneducated faithful in the typical black church. Every congregation marched on firmly to establish some form of church school. The facilities were as limited as the formal education of the teachers, but the "white folks" had established the model, and no self-respecting black church was without a Sunday school and, later, without an evening youth training group.

The movement among the untrained laity gained further momentum from the way it served the self-esteem of instructors. They saw themselves as teachers of the faith in a way which, so far as they could see, was not possible among the more educated. They seemed at the time to be unaware of the fact that the institutions of higher learning which were training the black elite were just as committed as they to "good religion," and to the Sunday School. There was a subtle assumption that to leave the culture of the masses was to leave the true faith. From this massive misunderstanding among both extremes came the Sunday School of the black masses, marked by astounding investments of energy, dedication, and racial and personal pride. Yet the learning was limited to just such healthy self-esteem and the rudiments of rote religious materials such as the books of the Bible and the magnificent collection of stories. This zealous endeavor, with its short classes and long assemblies, represents a tradition of Sunday Schools which even now, a century later, dies hard.

What was the net effect of this massive movement? The answer has to be that it was a mixed blessing. On the positive side, there can be no doubt that the rapid and solid growth of the black churches in the reconstruction era and the decades following was in part due to the organizing impact of the Sunday School movement. Again, the "track record" of leaders developed in Sunday Schools is most impressive. The "superintendent" of the local Baptist Sunday School in any town was an important personage, and often still is. Many a mature black still remembers with pride an Easter recitation or a Christmas play which awakened his or her first conscious awareness of personal dignity and worth.

The importance of these public appearances can hardly be overestimated. William Holtzclaw, born about 1870, tells of such an experience:

> The next night we said our little pieces, and I suppose we looked about as well as the others; at least, we thought so, and that was sufficient. One thing I am sure of—there was no mother there who was prouder of her children than ours.[15]

Perhaps the crowning contribution of the Sunday Schools would have to be the tremendous percentage of black adult Christians whose sense of identity with and commitment to Jesus Christ was evidenced and symbolized in a conversion experience during childhood or youth. Almost all of these were directly or indirectly the result of the love, concern, and influence of teachers in the Sunday Schools, and of the joyous activities associated with this program.

On the other hand, the current decline of the Sunday School among blacks reflects internal flaws as well as external influences and negative trends. This is best illustrated by comparison of the high and often rising numbers in attendance at the public worship in some black churches while their church schools experience a decided decline in attendance. If the tremendous tradition of dedication to Christian education is to be saved among the black churches, we must acknowledge a series of major errors and face the fact that the black church school movement has succeeded, at least partially, in spite of rather than because of many of its practices.

The first major error would seem to be at the bottom of many of the others: black Sunday Schools were altogether too dependent on the externals of early white Sunday Schools as a model. These reflected none of the unique styles and needs of blacks. Rather, they emphasized gimmicks and whoopla such as competition for attendance and offering banners. These were the pride and joy of a middle-class religiosity committed to a culture of fierce competition in business and industry. It bore little resemblance to the extended-family mentality of African-Americans, but they bought it hook, line, and sinker. In their eagerness to give their young the best, they forgot that "white is not always right" either educationally or spiritually.

As noted already, black and white Sunday Schools were the proud domain of the laity, a volunteer crew intentionally innocent of professional insights and qualifications. With the successful emphasis on bigness came a predictable drop in the quality of instruction. Although their dedication was high, their educational orientation was low, and their not-unimpressive achievements were in spite of their theories. A 1969 dissertation by Margaret Sawin would cause one to suspect that (white) Sunday School teachers had even lower-than-average intellectual and emotional development.[17] Black churches copied the former if not the latter, of necessity perhaps rather than choice. Denominational publishing houses which sought to raise lay levels of insight in either group soon "lost a bundle." Some members of white denominations went so far as to withdraw from their communions, alleging deviation from the faith. The real issue, however, no doubt included resistance to materials that forced teachers to do some thinking for themselves. Most Sunday School teachers, of whatever ethnic group, still want a cut-and-dried, simplistic lesson plan.

Blacks were once known for mixing their weekday skills-learning with Sunday's Bible lessons in an effort to "catch up." They were once gifted with indigenous talents for teaching, but they slowly surrendered their historic methods and relevance to the needs of black liberation in an effort to conform. Thus, unwittingly, they joined an antiintellectual swing to mediocrity in the American Sunday School movement. As it served the ego strivings of the majority, so did it serve black needs for even a little bit of recognition. Teacher self-esteem may have prospered, but pupil learning languished.

Another interesting flaw shared by black and white was the strange fascination with burgeoning buildings—monuments to the pride of both clergy and laity. The irony among blacks was that once the building had been erected and the notes paid off, the use of the building was still at least one-hundred years behind the times. The victory in dealing with financial problems only served, all too often, to uncover the severe limitations of the teacher. There was a time when classes were too brief for the teacher to have much to say. There were also other classes in the same auditorium, and much of what the teacher did say could be devoted simply to keeping order. The "assembly hour" also took up entirely too much time with petty details. But it helped disguise the limitations of the teacher. Then came the assignment of an individual classroom; the longer private teaching time was shattering to teacher and pupil alike. Time could no longer be frittered away with reclaiming attention from the surrounding activities. Children both missed the fun of watching other classes in movement, and finally had to see just how dull the lessons were. In a sense, the new buildings made more problems rather than solving them. There were teachers who resigned outright because the new classroom put too many demands on them, although they gave other reasons for leaving.

However, perhaps the most damaging of all errors copied from others was the exaggerated fascination with print. It implied that there was no further need for the powerful oral tradition. Both blacks and whites developed a dependency on brief, printed commentaries, adding little or nothing of their own in class sessions. The pretty cards or leaflets were supposed to do the work of instruction, and there was little or no creativity or relation to real-life experiences. Old-time conversations in context, like Jesus' pointing out the lilies in the fields or Uncle Remus referring to the common rabbit, were seldom used to make the lesson stick and come alive.

To end the review on a positive note, it is undeniable that the most positive influence in the midst of all these negatives was the fact that the Sunday School provided so many activities and relationships apart from formal instruction. These were all opportunities for self-expression in a world where few such openings existed. This analysis suggests, at the same time, a partial explanation as to why the Sunday School in the black community has fallen on evil days. The external pressures which forced blacks to intense relationship and interaction no longer exist, or certainly not to the same extent. There are among blacks far more options for entertainment and movement as well as a wider range of possible relationships. The contemporary black church has thus been forced to make some serious changes and consider some radically different alternatives.

In the chapter which is scheduled to follow in due time, these responses will be surveyed and evaluated. Meanwhile, suffice it to say that the plight of nurture in the black churches and communities is that its best days thus far lie in the distant past. The most effective teaching and learning occurred at precisely the least promising time. The survival and sanity, the faith and perseverance, of millions of black and oppressed are mute testimony to a system of instruction well worth this historical examination and much more. To forget the great strengths to the golden age of the black churches' productivity in the reconstruction era would not only be a terrible affront to the black ancestors; it would be a tragic waste of spiritual and cultural resources, for which blacks and all other human beings have a special need today.

Notes

1. John S. Mbiti, *African Religions and Philosophy* (New York: Preager, 1969), p. 275.

2. Herbert V. Klem, *Oral Communication of the Scripture: Insights from African Oral Art* (Pasadena, Calif.: William Carey Library, 1982), p. 118.

3. Ibid., p. 127.

4. Ibid., p. 134

5. Isaac O. Delano, *Yoruba Proverbs* (Ibadan, Nigeria: Oxford University Press, 1966), p. 109.

6. E. B. Idowu, *Olodumare: God in Yoruba Belief* (London: Longman, 1962), p. 138. See also Fadipe, p. 270 ff. and Mbiti, p. 177.

7. Klem, *Oral Communication,* p. xv.

8. Henry H. Mitchell, *Black Belief* (New York: Harper & Row, 1975), n.p.n.

9. George P. Rawick ed. *The American Slave: A Composite Autobiography,* vol. 18 (Westport, Conn.: Greenwood Publishing Co., 1972), p. 284.

10. John W. Blassingame, *The Slave Community* (New York: Oxford University Press, 1972), p. 79.

11. Rawick, *The American Slave,* vol. 3, p. 205.

12. Rawick, vol. 6, p. 271.

13. Rawick, vol. 18, p. 189.

14. James D. Tyms, *The Rise of Religious Education Among Negro Baptists* (New York: Exposition Press, 1965), pp. 157-161.

15. Jay David, *Growing Up Black* (New York: William Morrow and Co., Inc., 1968), p. 139.

16. Nichols, n.p., 1987, pp. 185-187.

17. Margaret Sawin, "A Study of Sunday School Teachers' Personality Characteristics and Attitudes Toward Children," doctoral dissertation, University of Maryland, 1969.

4
Worship in the Black Church
Dearing E. King

There is no such thing as a "black church" or a "white church." If you will agree with me on that, then I will agree with you and use the terms to accommodate our abortive designations. With that understanding, let me restate the subject—"Worship in the Black Church."

Today when Christians are divided over most issues, there seems to be one point of unanimous agreement: we are headed in the wrong direction, and we are getting nowhere fast. Too long has our American church life, based on race, been expressed in the words of a disgusted pastor. After a stormy official board meeting, the pastor was called upon to close the meeting with prayer. In an atmosphere of confusion the veteran minister said: "Lord, as Thou hast blessed us in our coming together, bless us now as we come apart." That prayer would not be amiss for our dilemma as we confess that we cannot actually sing: "We are not divided;/All one body we." With that admission, it is my prayer and hope that we might turn with an openness of heart, mind, and spirit in the right direction of togetherness.

Worship is the best place to begin. Since worship is the central act of the church of Jesus Christ, we may well perceive the divine judgment upon the distorted image of Christ on the American form of Christianity. The true image of Christ has been defaced, which makes the American church life a mere form of godliness. Therefore, this form needs to be reminted so that Christ's image might be restored. "For the time is come," said the apostle Peter, "that judgment must begin at the house of God" (1 Pet. 4:17).

Without looking again at the scandal of separation between the races in American church life, it would be impossible to understand the uniqueness of worship in the black church. You see, worship may be defined as a spontaneous consciousness of God's presence. Hence a public service of worship itself should be a corporate experience, a prayerful togetherness. Such an act of corporate worship takes place whenever worshipers of various backgrounds, points of view, social and individual differences assemble together to affirm their personal identities in an authentic sharing of God's presence, grace, power, will, and purpose for the betterment of their own lives and for others. When this cannot be accomplished so that our lives may level off to a common Christian brotherhood, then the left-out person or group has to seek other worship arrangements. That accounts for: "Worship in the Black Church."

Worship and Self-realization

For a meaningful understanding of worship in the black church, let us begin with the black thrust for self-realization. Because black peole were locked out from the in-white-group everywhere else, they felt that their last resort was the white church, since that was the only church existing during the time of slavery. For some unknown reason, blacks could be fooled about everything else except the church of the Lord Jesus Christ. Even their white slave masters taught them that the church is a body of baptized believers in Christ. It is a community of the committed. Hence, black people bent over backwards in an effort to be accepted into the white church which was the only Christian community that they knew about. But for more than three-hundred years the white church has been more concerned with immunity than with community, with disaffiliation than with reconciliation. As a result, for the most part, blacks have been denied the right and privilege of participation in the white church. From slavery until now, blacks have been humiliated, embarrassed, harrassed, brutally attacked, arrested, and imprisoned for even attempting to worship in white churches of all denominations. Even when they were admitted to worship and membership in a few white churches, they were relegated to the rear or to the balconies. They were also forced to wait until whites were served the Lord's Supper before they were served.

From the treatment suffered by blacks in the white church it is indeed a miracle that they did not renounce Christianity altogether. Perhaps they would have if they had not psychologically separated Christ from the white church. Even by the simplest approach to Christian understanding, it was utterly impossible for the most insensitive to tolerate such racist, unchristian acts of worship in the house of God.

Out of that scandal of separation, the black church came into being as a thrust of black people for self-realization. They asked the question with the apostle Paul: "Is Christ divided?" (1 Cor. 1:13). Their answer was in leaving the white church. That was the only way they could be a part of the local body of Christ, since they could could not find acceptance within the white church. Otherwise, there would have been a stunting of the moral and spiritual growth of black believers if they had remained within the dehumanizing and depersonalizing structure of white American "churchianity." Their only option for self-realization was to originate their own place of worship where they could express their faith. From this place developed the unique distinctives of worship in the black church.

Worship and Unwavering Faith

One basic distinction is an unwavering faith in the absolute sovereignty of the supreme, infinite Creator. This faith must have been mysteriously and miraculously delivered to black people. They could not read, nor were there schools for them to attend. They had no persons or institutions to which they could look or on which they could depend for relief, religiously or legally, including the United States government.

More strange still was the ability of blacks to identify themselves with the Hebrews who had been in similar bondage under Pharaoh in Egypt and how they had tried to liberate themselves to no avail. The Hebrews came to the point of no return. In their extremity, God revealed Himself to Moses in absolute, divine sovereignty, saying:

> I have surely seen the affliction of my people which are in Egypt, and have heard their cry by reason of their taskmasters; for I know their sorrows; And I am come down to deliver them out of the hand of the Egyptians, and to bring them up out of that land unto a good land and large, unto a land flowing with milk and honey (Ex. 3:7-8).

This absolute sovereign Power is the basis for worship in the black church. In short, there is no more sublime fact in the history and experience of the black church than her steady, unwavering faith in the absolute sovereignty of God. This anchored faith in the Eternal was strangely delivered to black slaves, and they religiously transmitted it, through worship, to successive generations. From that immovable sovereign base, black people have always had room enough to sing and shout from earth to heaven.

Yes, through divine providence the absolute sovereign power of God was revealed to black people among the bulrushes of the Nile River where God's chosen people had been stripped of their freedom and reduced to oppressive slavery in Egypt. There blacks established identity with the Hebrews and connected that divine sovereignty to the black plantation soil along the Mississippi River to which they had been taken from their African homeland and reduced from persons to property. There, amid inhuman conditions and animalistic treatment, they got a glimpse of the Almighty which was revealed in a stable in Bethlehem.

That connection, from the bulrushes on the Nile River to the little Jesus boy, born in a manger, has been the sovereign key by which black people have entered humble places of worship and built altars as they lifted their voices with David in this psalm of praise: "The earth is the Lord's, and the fulness thereof; the world, and they that dwell therein" (Ps. 24:1). Or, as Deacon Terry Rogers used to pray: " 'From everlasting to everlasting'; from way back beyond back; before there was a when or a where, or a then or a there; You stepped out from nowhere and stood on nothing, and said, Let there be; and worlds leaped from Your presence like sparks from a blacksmith's anvil. Then You left word that whenever I needed You to call You. Lord, I need You now because I have no one else to turn to." After Brother Rogers's prayer the choir would march in singing, "Holy! Holy! Holy! there is none beside Thee." The pastor always closed the worship with this benediction: "Now unto the only wise God, our Father . . ."

This unwavering faith in the absolute sovereignty of the supreme, infinite Creator is the key to worship in the black church. Because black people have been cramped into oppressive, socially structural confinement, their very existence has demanded that they would give their devotion to the sovereign Supreme Being outside of themselves. When black people meet to worship their sovereign Lord, it is because they know through faith that only He could unify their disconnected, disorganized, and fragmented existence.

Worship and Spiritual Creativity

Another distinction of black church worship is spiritual creativity. Here we see worship as a contradistinction to worship in white churches. The very use of the terms *white church* and *black church* is an obvious admission that the church has practiced birth control; and in the process, it has become spiritually uncreative and unproductive. In the very nature of the church of Christ, the purpose of authentic worship is to bring worshipers into a conscious relationship with God and into a spiritual relationship with all believers in Christ. Through worship, people may be directed in their quest for the reality of God and for the fellowship of kindred minds as "like to that above." This is a spiritually creative experience in the black church. Its worship deals primarily with the only two realities: God and people—all people. This spiritual, social, fellowship edifies common humanity. For these reasons, true worship reaches its highest expression in mutual group sharing.

For instance, black people have always realized there can be no genuine worship experience based upon the sovereign power of God alone. Authentic worship in the church of Jesus Christ must include both God and neighbor. This is mandatory for spiritual creativity in the life of the church and for a sense of eternal life in each believer. This is what the parable of the good Samaritan is all about. The activities of the Jewish priest and Levite were about religion, while the spiritual creativity of the good Samaritan was about life. This is the reason why new, creative life was generated in the man who had fallen among thieves and was stripped, beaten, and left half dead.

The reason spiritual creativity is noticeable in black church worship is that worshipers are actually involved with God and neighbor. From its inception, the black church has had no policy denying either membership or seating to people because of skin color, creed, or station in life. Without the involvement of both God and neighbor, no institution or organization can even be labeled as the church of Jesus Christ.

Because worship in the black church involves both God and neighbor, there is a freedom of expression and movement that is not of this world. This enables black congregations to transcend time, place, and conditions. A white pastor said to a black pastor, "Why do you hold services so long?" The black pastor answered: "We wait until the Holy Spirit comes. But you miss the Holy Spirit because you spend more time getting out of church than you do getting in."

Worship in the black church is not subject to any rigid rule of order. The main features of the service are singing, praying, preaching, and giving. In many instances, much time is taken for announcements.

Worship in the Black Church 75

This is necessary because the black church through its spiritual creativity gave birth to many black organizations, business, and movements. Therefore, time has to be allowed to promote the work of such agencies as the NAACP, the Urban League, the Southern Christian Leadership Conference, black newspapers, and so forth. These agencies have fought for black causes when the white church and the federal government failed to do so.

I believe no church has experienced music, instrumentally and otherwise, as is creatively rendered in the black church. Listen, if you please, to a black organist or pianist, and you will agree that the instrumentalist is creatively reaching for the lost chord. The instrumentalist plays people into breathless ecstasy. Listen to the singing. Musicians and singers creatively improvise, composing something brand-new out of old tunes. They may sing a song through for two or three times and repeat the refrain indefinitely without conveying a sense of routine or boredom. Often, they make up songs and tunes on the spot. This is spiritual creativity of the first magnitude.

Without question, preaching in the black church is the main feature of worship. There is absolutely nothing in heaven or on earth like a black preacher. If he is a Baptist preacher, you may double the dose. His contribution to black people in particular and to Americans in general can never be adequately appraised. He has literally stood with the prophet Ezekiel in the valley of dry bones with an optimism and a gospel of hope that must be a mystery that angels desire to look into. He is not merely a reciter of nothings, making acrobatic movements to draw attention to himself. When he stands up to preach, he should be fully conscious of his God-appointed ministry to teach the wandering, the wayward, the lonely, the oppressed, the depressed, and the lost into the secret place of the "Most High." For this purpose, he should be primarily involved in the drama of divine redemption.

For instance, when black slaves were not allowed to congregate or to communicate in groups, the black preacher, who had to keep his identity as a preacher concealed, devised ways of preaching to the slaves. He would tell the water boy to announce the service at a given time by singing through the fields: "Steal Away." All of the slaves knew to go to the swampy forest that night for worship. Another slave would be stationed at the big house to ascertain whether or not the acts of worship could be heard. The next morning he went through the fields singing, "O, I couldn't hear nobody pray."

When the slave preacher gave such a vivid description of Christ, His birth, His life, His death, resurrection, and ascension, blacks knew that he could not read; so they asked him in the words of the spiritual: "Were you there when they crucified my Lord?"

Take for example, the late John Jasper of Old Sixth Mount Zion Baptist Church of Richmond, Virginia. It is said that on one Easter Sunday morning, he was preaching and demonstrating how Jesus raised Lazarus from the grave. In the balcony was a white student from the Richmond Union Seminary with his son. John Jasper created an almost visible grave as he had Jesus bring Lazarus forth. Several times he said, "Jesus said to Lazarus, 'Come forth!' " The student's little boy said, "Daddy, come, let's go." The student and the congregation were transfixed as Jasper had Jesus bring Lazarus forth. Finally, the son got up and said, "Daddy, let's go before he makes the man get up." That is spiritual creativity when a preacher is able to raise the dead on Sunday morning!

Quite obviously, creativity in worship is woven into the total religious experience of the black church. This is evident even in funeral services. As a boy in the country, I recall worship experiences at funerals. There were no doleful singing, read prayers, and soulless eulogies. At that time, rural congregations had not even heard of the term *eulogy*. The preacher's message was always called the sermon. Except for the body in the casket and the bereaved family, the services were similar to those on Sundays. For instance, at one funeral the bereaved family had experienced other drastic losses. The minister in his introduction referred to the element of tragedies which the family had suffered. Then he called attention to the uncompared losses of

Job, including the deaths of all his children caused by a storm that wrecked the house where they were feasting. Then he took this text: "Then Job arose, and rent his mantle, and shaved his head, and fell down upon the ground, and worshipped" (Job 1:20). At the close of the sermon, the attendants had forgotten all about their losses.

Again at Pine Hill Baptist Church of La Grange, Tennessee, where I was converted and baptized, the pastor, Rev. Petsy Brown, preached the funeral of Sister Nancy Bailey. When he described heaven with jasper walls, streets of gold, gates of pearl, sea of glass, and the heavenly host, which no one could number, people were spellbound. Then he concluded with Jesus on His throne surrounded by twenty-four elders clothed in white raiment, and on their heads were crowns of gold. The sermon was so climactically worshipful that the congregation left the church feeling that it was a shame not to be dead.

In the beginning of my ministry, I experienced the contrast between types of funeral messages—eulogy and sermon. Some friends lost their mother in Maro, Arkansas, a rural community. Because they did not want to be stirred from the effects of the gospel, they requested the pastor to invite me to deliver the eulogy. Calmly and methodically, I depicted the mother's life as a beautiful and serviceable person. The family and congregation quitely nodded approval with smiles. At the end of the eulogy, the presiding pastor arose and said: "Anybody who has served the Lord for forty-seven years, as this sister, the funeral ought to be preached. Therefore, my text is found in Job 14:14—'If a man die, shall he live again?' " Within seven minutes he had people standing, rejoicing, and shouting all over the place. I have not attempted to do a eulogy since. The listing of my funeral message on the program is not eulogy but The Gospel.

The creative reenactment of the divine act of redemption has brought about the most unique and effective ministry in the world. Through preaching, black preachers have vindicated the faith which Christ pledged by giving them a place when they and their people were left out of the existing church life. Certainly, Christ must repeat

Himself as He sees black preachers lifting congregations from despair, sin, and death as He said to the seventy-two: "I beheld Satan as lightning fall from heaven" (Luke 10:18).

Through the spiritual creativity of worship in the black church, blacks can boast with John that "now are we the sons of God, and it doth not yet appear what we shall be" (1 John 3:2).

Worship as Celebration

This brings us to the final distinction of worship in the black church. It is the act of celebration. This call to celebration is with such unrehearsed and undirected joyful enthusiasm that it has amazed all other churches looking in from the outside. What is it, you ask, that makes black people so joyful, so supremely happy? Why do they make so much noise over Christ and their newfound joy in their Lord? What is it that holds them in church all day on Sunday from week to week?

Black congregations meet to celebrate the sovereignty of God. When you see them falling into one another's arms and shouting "Glory, Hallelujah," they are not exercising any more than the children of Israel did when God led them through the Red Sea. That was no time to be quiet. It was time to celebrate, so they broke out with a shout: "The Lord is my strength and song, and he is become my salvation: . . . The Lord is a man of war: the Lord is his name" (Ex. 15:2-3). The triumphant entry of Jesus to Jerusalem to announce His reign as King did not inspire frozen silence. It was a call to celebration, and "the multitudes that went before, and that followed, cried, saying, Hosanna to the son of David: Blessed is he that cometh in the name of the Lord; Hosanna in the highest" (Matt. 21:9).

Consider this triumphant note of praise. When God had wrought a great victory for black people, they spontaneously sang, "Ride on, King Jesus, no man can hinder You."

This celebration in worship is at the heart of the black church, for it is the only act of worship that no other body claims or attempts in the black tradition and manner.

In the black church, worship is fundamentally the only important service of the week; for people meet to celebrate the sovereignty of God for who He is, for what He has done and is doing for them, and in gratitude for Christ in pledging His faith in them as His children. In the celebration they also meet to renew their pledge and commitment to Him.

They also meet to celebrate because the black church is a survival institution where all people may come into an open door that no man can shut. There was a time when black people could not enter through the doors of education, politics, and other fields, but the door of revelation has always been open to them. Perhaps no other race or people in the Christian era has shared John's position on the Isle of Patmos more than black people. When the door of revelation was opened to John, the Isle of Patmos was no longer a desolate, uninhabitable place. As a matter of fact, John did not even acknowledge it as a place. He says: "I . . . was in the isle that is called Patmos" (1:9).

Since the late 1950s blacks have had similar experiences. Their thrust for self-realization in equality and justice in the total economy of this nation exposed them to some of the most vicious atrocities ever suffered by a people. But through the doors of black churches and, thank God, a few white churches, all people, black, white, red, and polka-dotted, participated in sit-ins, wade-ins, march-ins, and jail-ins. For the first time in American history, Dr. Martin Luther King, Jr., led people through blood, tears, and even death out of the fear of police and imprisonment. It was merely an isle that was called Patmos. This called for celebration even at the funeral of Dr. King.

No other people, except the Jews, have withstood so much for so long. It is, indeed, a great tribute to the black church that black people have been able to survive. Even the waiting has been a source of celebration.

The genius of the black church has been in its ability to accelerate time by celebrating things hoped for, the evidence of things not seen. Although Abraham did not actually see the realization of his desire

80 Black Church Life-Styles

as a fact, Jesus says: "Abraham rejoiced to see my day: and he saw it" (John 8:56). Through worship, blacks have always been able to celebrate their potential as a reality. Dr. Martin Luther King, Jr., said that when he boarded a segregated bus in Atlanta, Georgia, before he would take a seat in the rear assigned to blacks, he would always make his *mind* sit on the front seat. That was celebration of things hoped for. In worship, blacks have always known that the day would come when this nation would have black mayors, black congressmen, black state senators and legislators, black sheriffs, black judges, and so forth.

I remember a sermon preached by Petsy Brown when I was about seven years old. When he got through describing what we shall be, my mother pulled me into her arms and said: "Mamma's little boy is going to be president of these United States." You see, we do not celebrate what has happened; we celebrate our potential with the God of beginning again. This always keeps us on tiptoe to announce the wondrous surprise of what is to be and to redress the balance of the past. For blacks, the future has always infringed upon the present in worship. Therefore, we know that it is a present now and that it can only be shared when it is celebrated.

In worship, blacks actually embrace the Kingdom, which is Christ invisibly present in his church. There they know that they live in a Kingdom that is not of this world. Like the Jews, who constituted the wheel in the middle of the big Babylonian wheel, blacks constitute the wheel in the big American wheel. But unlike the Jews, who could not sing the Lord's song in a strange land, blacks can sing, pray, preach, and give to celebrate their victory that overcomes the world.

We do not celebrate, however, as an end in itself. Our goal is Christ Himself who loved us and gave Himself for us. I think Dr. Raymond Henderson sums this up for us. One day, he was preparing a sermon at the end of a hallway. His son kept coming down to the end of the hall and, although he said nothing, his presence was annoying. Twice he gave the boy money to go out and get candy or something from the store, but each time the boy would return and stand near his desk.

Finally Dr. Henderson said, "Bill, tell me, what do you want?" Billy's simple reply was: "Nothing! I just want to be near you."

Worship in the black church is like that. We do not assemble to air the grievances, the scandal of separation, or the atrocities of the past. We meet to worship for self-realization that we may be all that Christ intends for us to be as children of God. With unwavering faith in the absolute sovereignty of the Almighty, we worship as confirmed witnesses of our own spiritual creative originality and productivity. We meet to recommit ourselves to the supreme, infinite Creator who is able to keep us from falling and to present us faultless before the presence of His glory with exceeding joy. For that reason, we worship to celebrate, not only because of the things that are come to pass, but because of the things that are yet to come. We celebrate to reaffirm our faith in the assurance that the time shall come when all believers in Christ shall, everywhere, drop the color bar and triumphantly sing together "All one body we,/One in hope and doctrine,/One in charity." We shall also join the "great voices in heaven, saying, The kingdoms of this world shall become the kingdoms of our Lord, and of his Christ; and he shall reign for ever and ever" (Rev. 11:15). Then it shall come to pass as it was in the beginning, "When the morning stars sang together, and all the sons of God shouted for joy" (Job 38:7).

5
Black Hymnody
Wendel Whalum

The most important singular contribution of black people to the making of American culture is their music. Rooted as it is in every fiber of a certain black life-style, it may reflect at its depths a deep sense of longing due to poor social conditions which life imposes, or it may at its height rise to a level of great hope. The sense of longing indicates that blacks never accepted their plight or had the slightest intentions of being satisfied with it. The level of hope musically expressed itself in thoughts of joy, happiness, and expectation that dispelled gloom. This is especially true in the period of the "oral tradition" which was strongest until the late 1860s.

The oral tradition represents that period when, with no formal or academic training, blacks developed their own methods of dealing with the realities of American life. Although expressed musically, the Bible became a primary source for documenting their plight. It provided the textual material for the religious music which is at the very base of a consideration of black hymnody. The accounts of Moses, Jeremiah, Elijah, Ezekiel, Daniel, John, Matthew, Mark, Luke, and others take on more significance when interpreted against the backdrop of eighteenth- and nineteenth-century human bondage. They, and their inspiration, live again in this spiritual music. Through such vivid imagination as the spiritual affords, a boldness in spirit is girded by a faith which becomes an unfailing anchor.

Several writers have raised doubts as to the authenticity of the spiritual as well as all other oral literature of black people. Since notable responses have been made to these, we will not deal with the subject here. Harold Courlander has written a valid response to their charges in *Negro Folk Music, U.S.A.:*

> Any notion that Negro oral religious literature is primitive or naive . . . an impression conveyed by numerous literary treatments . . . certainly does not survive careful reading or hearing. The song "All God's Children Got Wings," far from being quaint or childlike, is an expression of faith couched in symbols that were apparent to most pre-literate slaves and, later, liberated Negroes. While some people must have taken the inherent promises of this song literally, for most Negroes the wings, harps, and shoes must have conveyed simply the idea of relief from a hard and unrewarding life, either in this world or another. If Negro religious imagery is truly "naive," then the burden of responsibility must be borne by the Bible, out of which the imagery is primarily extracted.
>
> Negro religious literature, like the secular, is marked by an economy of statement, rich and fresh scenes, and the capacity to evoke recognition and response. The entire story of Jonah is presented in a song of fourteen lines, every one of which is visual and dramatic. Many of the songs do not describe events so much as allude to them. Some telescope a variety of allusions into a few tight phrases.[1]

Spirituals have their roots in the eighteenth century when need among slaves for expression in a common language was strongest. The newly created music united the descendants of the various African tribes, who now had a common bond in slavery. It is, therefore, not music for the sake of music, but music which is reflective of the experiences of slaves and "freedmen" and music which is, in its most positive sense, communicative—one with the other as well as with the group. It is music that embraces, in varying degrees, the quest for life, love, identity, acceptance, sometimes death, and always, freedom. The quest is always there.

Accounts of religious music of the early years of the eighteenth century are scant and must be dealt with in generalities. But Dena J. Epstein[2] has provided an excellent article on the best of the very early sources.

Black hymnody, categorically speaking, must include all serious music that is sacred to the black experience. This should suggest all the serious music that falls within the boundaries of Christianity as it seized the black experience as well as that serious music which was sacred to the experience, but not necessarily Christian in nature. It is a point of wonder that, as far as we know, the music of blacks of pre-Christian days could be contained, intact, after the introduction of Christianity.

The serious sacred music of the oral tradition is primarily individual-to-group music. It begins with the individual but is made into final composition, finished, and polished by the group.

Those groups who made the music, before and since the Civil War, assembled to work at further definition of their faith and reviving their hope in a delivering God. They also took great pains to "count their blessings." In those meetings when music was sung, there were no observers. Everyone was a participant. An individual contributed a musical "thought," and the group worked it over and over, reshaping phrases, adding and subtracting notes, filling in melodic gaps, adjusting harmony and rhythm. Many spirituals died when they failed to do what the group intended them to do.

If a member of the group could not sing, he could pat his foot; if he could not pat, he could sway his head; and if he could not do this, he could witness. Everyone was expected to participate.

Another important factor here is that the black church never needed or had a choir. The choir was the entire congregation who, as James Weldon Johnson pointed out,[3] had able and talented musical leaders on whom the body of singers depended for musical guidance.

To sum it up, the spiritual became the musical basis for all later black church music.

One important point that must not escape the introductory lines of this work has to do with the particular group of blacks who prepared and preserved this music. It is this group that insisted, without full endorsement of the clergy, on taking the music from the slave quarter to the institutional church. It is they who, when warned against using this music in the church, found a place for it in prayer meetings, ring shouts, and services as well as in daily personal and community devotions. It is, therefore, to them that we must give the credit for the preservation of the older music types of which we have only a few examples. And today, isolated in storefront churches, rural towns, and sea islands, they continue to sing the music.

Expressed feelings against the use of spirituals, especially shouting ones, are evident from early black church fathers. The attitude of Richard Allen (1760-1831) is described as follows:

> From about 1800, Richard Allen published books of every sort for his parishioners, including hymn books. Some of the hymns he personally wrote. Some of his "spiritual songs" are quite conventional, in the tradition of the white spiritual. Others devote themselves to admonitions to improve the flock. For example, Richard Allen did not like shouting Methodists; he thus had his congregation sing,
>
> > "Such groaning and shouting, it sets me to doubting,
> > I fear such religion is only a dream;
> > The preachers are stamping, the people were jumping,
> > And screaming so loud that I neither could hear,
> > Either praying or preaching, such horrible screeching
> > 'Twas truly offensive to all that were there."
>
> The significant factor is that the hymn is directed toward the personal and group behavior of the people.[4]

The years accompanying the establishment of the institutional church are the years that began the cessation of the spiritual. The strongest blow, however, came from Daniel Payne, who thought that the imitation of established denominations was the best approach. In order to make his point, he honestly belittled those who practiced folklore in religious services.

Payne (1811-93), in his excellent document *Recollections of Seventy Years,* published in 1888, gave much helpful information along with the account of his attitude about the folk music to which we have referred. That aside, for the moment, let us consider these pertinent facts from his book:

> 1. The first introduction of choral singing into the African Methodist Episcopal Church took place in Bethel (Church), Philadelphia, Pa., between 1841-1842. It gave great offense to the older members, especially those who had professed personal sanctification. Said they: "You have brought the devil into the Church, and therefore we will go out."
>
> 2. "So great was the excitement and irritation produced by the introduction of the choir into Bethel Church that I, then a local preacher and schoolmaster, was requested by the leader of the choir and other prominent members in it to preach a special sermon on sacred music. This I did the best I could. In my researches I used a small monograph on music written by Mr. Wesley. . . . The immediate effect of that discourse was to check the excitement, soothe the irritation, and set the most intelligent to reading as they had never done before."
>
> 3. Instrumental music was introduced into our denomination in the year 1848-9. It commenced at Bethel, in Baltimore.[5]

Now let us return to the tongue-lashing that Bishop Payne gave a group that sang the folk music:

> I have mentioned the "Praying and Singing Bands" elsewhere. The strange delusions that many ignorant but well-meaning people labor under leads me to speak particularly of them. About this time I attended a "bush meeting," where I went to please the pastor whose circuit I was visiting. After the sermon they formed a ring, and with coats off sung, clapped their hands and stamped their feet in a most ridiculous and heathenish way. I requested the pastor to go and stop their dancing. At his request they stopped their dancing and clapping of hands, but remained singing and rocking their bodies to and fro. This they did

for about fifteen minutes. I then went, and taking their leader by the arm requested him to desist and to sit down and sing in a rational manner. I told him also that it was a heathenish way to worship and disgraceful to themselves, the race, and the Christian name. In that instance they broke up their ring; but would not sit down, and walked sullenly away. After the sermon in the afternoon, having another opportunity of speaking alone to this young leader of the singing and clapping ring, he said: "Sinners won't get converted unless there is a ring." Said I: "You might sing until you fell down dead and you would fail to convert a single sinner, because nothing but the Spirit of God and the word of God can convert sinners." He replied: "The Spirit of God works upon people in different ways. At camp-meeting there must be a ring here, a ring there, a ring over yonder, or sinners will not get converted." This was his idea, and it is also that of many others. These "Bands" I have had to encounter in many places, and, as I have stated in regard to my early labors in Baltimore, I have been strongly censured because of my efforts to change the mode of worship or modify the extravagances indulged in by the people. In some cases all that I could do was to teach and preach the right, fit, and proper way of serving God. To the most thoughtful and intelligent I usually succeeded in making the "Band" disgusting; but by the ignorant masses, as in the case mentioned, it was regarded as the essence of religion. So much so was this the case that, like this man, they believe no conversion could occur without their agency, nor outside of their own ring could any be a genuine one. Among some of the songs of the "Rings," or "Fist and Heel Worshipers," as they have been called, I find a note of two in my journal, which were used in the instance mentioned. As will be seen, they consisted chiefly of what are known as "cornfield ditties:"

> Ashes to ashes, dust to dust;
> If God won't have us, the devil must.
> I was way over there where the coffin fell;
> I heard that sinner as he screamed in hell.[6]

Fredrika Bremer (1801-65), a native of Sweden, wrote the following about the AME Church in Cincinnati in *Homes of the New World* (1853):

> Diary entry Columbia, South Carolina, May 25th, 1850—When at home with Mr. B., I heard the negroes singing, it having been so arranged by Hannah L. I wished rather to have heard their own naive songs, but was told that they "dwelt with the Lord" and sang only hymns. I am sorry for this exclusiveness; nevertheless, their hymns sung in quartette were glorious . . .
>
> Cincinnati, Ohio, November 27th, 1850—I had in the forenoon visited a negro Baptist church belonging to the Episcopal creed. There were but few present, and they of the negro aristocracy of the city . . . the hymns were beautifully and exquisitely sung.
>
> In the afternoon I went to the African Methodist Church in Cincinnati, which is situated in the African Quarter. . . . The singing ascended and poured forth like a melodious torrent, and the heads, feet, and elbows of the congregation moved all in unison with it, amid evident enchantment and delight in the singing, which was in itself exquisitely pure and full of melodious life.
>
> The hymns and psalms which the negroes have themselves composed have a peculiar naïve character, childlike, full of imagery and life. Here is a specimen of one of their popular church hymns:
>
>> What ship is this that's landed at the shore?
>> Oh, glory halleluiah!
>> It's the old ship of Zion, halleluiah;
>> It's the old ship of Zion, halleluiah.
>> Is the mast all sure, and the timber all sound?
>> Oh, glory halleluiah!
>> She's built of gospel timber, halleluiah;
>> etc., etc.
>
> After the singing of the hymns, which was not led by any organ or musical instrumental whatever, but which arose like burning melodious sighs from the breasts of the congregation, the preacher mounted the pulpit.[7]

These accounts help explain why the religious folk music of slaves and former slaves faded into the background after the first sixty-five or so years of the nineteenth century. Perhaps it was time for this music to be halted, and perhaps it was true that, if blacks were to worship in a nation that recognized hymn books, choirs, and organs as necessary entities of the worship service, they should fully understand these aids. But the development progressed, obstinately, to another rather interesting state. While the Methodists were, more or less according to the presiding bishop, attempting to get in step with England's gift to the religious practices of the New World, the Baptists in no real uniformity were, in the words of Joseph Washington, "slower in developing a structure due to the local autonomy of each congregation."[8] The truth is that Baptists allowed for more individual participation and address to church affairs than the Methodists. The Baptists, therefore, are responsible for developing a "new" kind of singing that utilized the "new" hymn texts in a manner unique to most black Baptist congregations.

The following account is invaluable in understanding why the spiritual was gradually replaced by hymns in the sacred service. Eileen Southern gave the account of the era as follows:

During the 1730s a new religious movement swept the [New England and Middle] colonies, the so-called "Great Awakening," bringing with it a demand for the use of livelier music in the worship service. The "new" songs of the movement were *hymns;* for text they employed religious poems instead of the scriptural psalms. In 1707 Dr. Isaac Watts, an English minister and physician, published a book, *Hymns and Spiritual Songs,* that became immensely popular in the colonies, especially among the black folk, because of the freshness and vitality of the words. In 1717 he published another collection of his attractive hymns, entitled *The Psalms of David, Imitated in the Language of the New Testament and Apply'd to the Christian State and Worship.* Before long, people began to neglect the psalms, preferring to sing hymns instead, especially since the latter were fitted to lively tunes. Slowly, the various Protestant denominations in the colonies, one after the other, adopted the hymns of Watts. The "Era of Watts" in the history of American religious music had begun.[9]

The black Methodists and Baptists endorsed Watts's hymns, but the Baptists "blackened" them. They virtually threw out meter and rhythm and, before 1875, had begun a new system which, though based on the style of singing coming from England to America in the eighteenth century, was drastically different from it. It was congregational singing much like the spiritual had been in which the text was retained. The melody sung in parallel intervals, fourths and fifths, sometimes thirds and sixths at cadence points, took a rather crudely shaped line which floated melismatically along, being held together primarily by the deacon who raised and lined it. It was this kind of singing that the white minister Charles A. Raymond wrote about in *Harper's New Monthly Magazine* in 1863. He entitled his account, "The Religious Life of the Negro Slave." In it he wrote about a service of worship as follows:

> In the Churches of the cotton-growing States the negro deacon is no unimportant personage. He is a pastor without being a preacher; and is also the connecting official link between his colored brethren in the church and their white associates. What the white pastor can never know, concerning the moral and social characters of the colored flock, the negro deacon can know. . . . Nothing was more suggestive than a meeting for the election of a deacon. . . . In meetings where business is to be transacted, the pastor is necessarily present. . . . He . . . calls upon the singers for a hymn, and the meeting is regularly organized. The usual devotional exercises, prayer and singing, occupy about half an hour. These are generally conducted by the negroes—the pastor being a quiet participator in the worship.

What the gentleman did not make clear, but is nevertheless the practice, is that the devotional exercises which he described are conducted by the deacons. One need only to visit some Baptist churches today, to discover the method outlined herein. In the service, that is, after the devotions, hymns are sung faithful to the score. In lining, the deacon gives out two lines of the hymn at a time and then leads the congregation in singing. Though the congregation is used to the method and the text, they enjoy and follow this practice as it has been done in the past. When the deacon motions for the congregation to stand, it is understood that the current stanza will be the concluding one. Most of the hymns sung in this manner are hymns of Dr. Watts. A substantial number of black Baptist churches have "Dr. Watts choirs" as a regular part of their musical offering in divine worship services.

The "Dr. Watts" hymns gave way in the late nineteenth century to a still more varied and interesting type known as shape-note singing. In this type a "professor" teaches "singing classes" the method of singing note shapes with their names, do, re, mi, etc. This use of syllables, attractive as it is, has led singing choirs into using the syllables for the first portion of their musical offering in services of worship. A few bodies of worshipers, especially the Church of Christ and Holiness groups, will use the notes for teaching purposes only and will not sing the notes by syllables in the services.

They do maintain the strict square rhythm that they took over from the great white gospel singers of the turn of the century, but the boldness of their voices almost makes one believe that the music, though it is not, is the work of black composers. Blacks, though, never assumed the authorship of them. They have been accused of such. The truth is that the softback books that contain this music are usually owned by those who sing from them and are not, usually, the property of the church in which they are heard.

When Christianity seized the black experience, the worshipers took hold of whatever was shared with them and made it into a music of their own. This was not plagiarism. It was an honest effort to give God their best. Many spirituals of this period became a part of many hymns. Two immediately come to mind:

(1) *Spiritual Refrain:*
He didn't have to wake me, but He did.
He didn't have to wake me, but He did.
Woke me up this morning, and started me on my way.
He didn't have to wake me, but He did.
Verse: (from a hymn)
Amazin' Grace, How sweet the sound,
That saved a wretch like me,
I once was lost, but now I'm found,
Was blind but now I see.

(2) *Spiritual Refrain:*
I got to lie down,
How shall I rise?
I got to lie down,
How shall I rise?
'Got to lie down,
How shall I rise?
'Pear fore the judgment bar.
Verse: (from a hymn)
Dark was the night and
Cold the ground
On which my Lord was laid.
Great drops of blood
Like sweat rolled down
In agony He prayed.

Following the second half of the nineteenth century, this method of singing, plus the already-mentioned "deaconed" ones, took hold, and the Baptists and probably only a few Methodists made it into what is still, today, one of the most beautiful and moving congregational musical offerings to be witnessed. In it there are no musical instruments and, usually, no hand clapping, though there is always the necessary steady pat of the foot on the carpetless floor of the church. It is also sometimes extremely difficult to understand what words are being sung since many singers slide over the words saving the vowel sounds for use with the notes. One interested in this aspect of black singing should certainly read John Work's article, "Plantation Meistersinger," in *The Music Quarterly*.[10] Though the texts are from hymnbooks, the music is unquestionably black.

One thing that must be said is that the music of the oral tradition was a utilitarian music, that is, it aimed at usefulness rather than beauty. It served the needs of the makers. It also reveals, in a peculiar period beginning about 1800, that the minds of the makers of the music were extremely clever and keen in perceiving an increased manner of communication with their fellows.

The insurrections that are well known occurred during the period when blacks from the North and black preachers in the South spoke a rebellious gospel, rooted in the Scriptures, to slaves. They were quite successful before being caught. They had a music to accompany it. It was religious music, honest and useful. It braved their hearts and minds and assured their souls that their efforts were at least right in the sight of God. Invoking God's blessing is an inseparable part of much of these "protest" songs. One is:

> Guide my feet, while I run this race (repeated 3 times)
> For I don't want to run this race in vain.

The late Miles Mark Fisher and the late John W. Work differed on its place of origin, but agreed that "Steal Away to Jesus" was a signal song for preparation meetings. A very telling one is:

> Get you ready, There's a meeting' here tonight
> Come along, There's a meetin' here tonight,
> I know you by your daily walk
> There's a meetin' here tonight.

Another famous one is:

> Walk together Children, don't you get weary
> There's a great camp meetin' in the Promised Land.

Another one, less famous, is from South Georgia, around Cordele:

> Don't say nothing
> Can't you hear?
> Don't do nothing
> Can't you hear?
> Standin' there behind you
> Lookin' this way,
> Don't say nothing
> Can't you hear?
>
> [Verse]
> One man in the wilderness
> One man gone to pray
> One man gon' go on home
> An' run til judgment day.
> Hallelujah!

And, of course, there were many more. But again, the marvel is that these, too, could be taken as they were for use in religious meetings with a real Christian motive behind them. That they had double meanings all the more underscores the clever mind of the slave. He knew that the master thought that "When they' singing, they' working."

Miles Mark Fisher[11] attempted a glossary of the meanings of some of the words frequently used in these spirituals. "Satan," says Fisher, is anyone who mistreated the slave. "King Jesus" was the slave's benefactor, "Babylon" and "winter" were slavery, "hell" was being sold farther South, and "Jordan" was the first step toward freedom. Fisher quotes V. F. Calverton, from an article entitled "The Negro and American Culture,"[12] who wrote that "there is more, far more than the ordinary Christian zeal embedded in Negro spirituals. They are not mere religious hymns written or recited to sweeten the service or improve the ritual, they are the aching, poignant cry of an entire people."

Of form and style of the spirituals we have said little. John W. Work, in an address to the Hymn Society of America,[13] covered this subject completely.

Musical activity in black communities around the turn of the century was more secular than sacred in nature. Church music was now fairly well established in the singing of hymns with organ accompaniment as well as anthems. Traditional music, as we have stated, had its place assigned to devotional services which took place before Sunday morning services, in prayer meetings, and in weekly community devotions. The ministers frequently led a meter hymn or a spiritual before or during the sermon, a practice which continues until today.

A few churches with outstanding choirs completely threw out the meter hymns and traditional music and engaged in singing cantatas and taking part in music festivals. The greater musical activity, though by far, transpired in the musical theaters of New York and Chicago and in hotels and auditoriums in other cities where black composers were busy working out their scores for performances. Scott Joplin, Will Marion Cook, Eubie Blake, James Reese Europe, and W. C. Handy were among the most active.

In 1895, one of the most important events was the organization of the National Baptist Convention. The organization allowed for more association among the clergy and members of that denomination and offered the opportunity for increased activity among the musicians of the churches.

By 1930, a new approach to religious life had been firmly established in the Holiness churches. Music in these churches was, for the most part, sung in the manner of the oral tradition. Efforts to define their reason for being led some of the bodies to use instruments, encourage rhythmic clapping, holy dancing, and speaking in tongues. Instrumental improvisation in dance-band fashion, for use during the long periods of dancing, was also encouraged. Other Holiness churches, especially the Church of God, Holiness, had a musical hodgepodge in which old spirituals, shape-note hymns, a total of about five bravura anthems, shouting, but no dancing, provided the fare.

In a sense, we must give credit to the Holiness churches for extending the life of the music of the oral tradition. For during their long and important devotional periods, sometimes several per week, many old and sometimes unfamiliar spirituals may be heard. Another part of this life extension is the contribution of the Fisk Jublilee Singers who, as pacesetters in 1871, revealed to the world the effectiveness of spiritual arrangements.[14]

Many of the black college and university choirs, glee clubs, and quartets followed the Fisk lead and found audiences, both black and white, increasingly eager to hear their renditions of sacred and secular black music. The quartet feature was effective, and many quartets were formed. Quartet singing flourished until the 1950s in a very popular fashion. They sang spiritual arrangements but specialized in those spirituals that contained unusually long narratives. The "Samson" story in the spiritual "Witness for my Lord," the drama in "John Saw the Number," "Daniel in the Lion's Den," "Hebrew Children in the Fiery Furnace," "David and Goliath," and others were, in special church programs, shouting numbers. In theaters and auditoriums they were "show stoppers." Some of the quartets were of the "hip slapper" type, while others were not only artistic but made up of men with trained voices.

In 1914 R. Nathaniel Dett accomplished a major task. He wrote an anthem, the first, based on a spiritual. After publication, this anthem became a part of the repertory of almost every average-to-exceptional choir in the country. Based on the spiritual "Listen to the Lambs," it was very effective.[15] Dett employed the usual anthem quality but retained the spiritual flavor. He inspired other composers, many of whom were black, to write spiritual-based anthems which became the pride of collegiate and church choirs.

In 1916 Harry T. Burleigh made a similar contribution when he published a spiritual for solo voice, artistically arranged. Later, many composers followed their lead. James Weldon and J. Rosamond Johnson produced a collection in two different books of spirituals for the solo voice.[16] Hall Johnson began and fully developed his choir which sang his own arrangements primarily. Activities in other places, such as Tuskegee, Fisk, Atlanta, and the like, gave these arrangements wide and numerous performances.

There were, of course, other arrangers and/or composers such as John W. Work, Willis Laurence James, Clarence Cameron White, Frederick Hall, William L. Dawson, and Kemper Harreld who seriously worked at reclaiming as much of this music as possible. As it is to be expected, many white arrangers and a few black ones, too, issued the music without fully understanding the roots and, consequently, gave out many scores that misrepresent the purposes of certain numbers. It has often been surprising to audiences to learn that every black folk song with religious words was not intended or used for worship services. In fact, many of these contain a bit of humor which would never have been permitted in the services of worship. "Little David, play on your harp, hallelu" is a case in point.

The style of the spiritual is simple. The rhythm is most important and that, according to research of John W. Work, "may be slow and pounding" or "hard and driving." Of meter, Work said, "true spirituals are in either 2/4 or 4/4."[17] They are dignified gems, and of the serious ones, humor is not intended or expected. They lay claim to an interpretation rendered only as a result of a belief and a faith.

The spiritual, therefore, is the root and trunk of black music. Its influences are felt today in much that we hear.

In the 1930s, following the beginning of the great depression, another music came to the fore. Called by several scholars the "twentieth-century spiritual," gospel music was introduced and began its long, winding development. As a result of the impact of this period of want, Pearl Williams-Jones, in her study of Afro-American gospel music, has labeled *1900-30: Pre-Gospel Era.* She had this to say:

The rise of gospel music around 1930 is attributable to several sociological changes within the black community, foremost among which was the steady increase in migration from the South by blacks in search of greater economic opportunities and freedom. With these migrants came their religious traditions which found an outlet for expression in the various humble store fronts and small church buildings which some congregations could afford. E. Franklin Frazier, eminent sociologist of Howard University, has given a very vivid and detailed account of these black churches in his book, *Black Bourgeoisie.* The musical traditions of these various denominations were maintained in the more fundamentalist-type churches, providing the greatest opportunity for the seeds of gospel music to come into full bloom. This came about in those churches which were not geared to traditional liturgy and formality of religious worship—some Baptist, a few Methodist, and a majority of the Pentecostal or Holiness Churches. There was, and has been, an unquenchable thirst among these people for their own music which could express their innermost feelings about God, and their emotional involvement which was a part of this expression. The music at hand was an idiom with which they were all familiar and it could be created spontaneously. The preacher, the song leader, and congregation all shared equally in those creative moments.[18]

The first three decades of the century also saw the shift in the world of secular music from ragtime to blues, to the recording of the blues, and the introduction of jazz. In no small measure did these expressions have their effect on gospel music. In fact, one of the leaders in the gospel music movement, Thomas A. Dorsey (b. 1899), was active as a blues pianist and before 1919 had been one of the successful pianists in the South, especially in Atlanta.

Dorsey acknowledged that his greatest influence was from Dr. C. A. Tindley, a writer of a number of "soul-stirring" songs.[19] Tindley was in the group that included Dr. and Mrs. Townsend, E. W. D. Isaac, Lucie E. Campbell, and others. Their songs, not known as hymns, were issued in National Baptist Convention publications: *Carols of Glory, Gospel Pearls, Awakening Echoes,* and *The Baptist*

Standard Hymnal, and became the possession of scores of soloists and choirs. A few of them, notably "He'll Understand and Say Well Done" by Campbell, are still sung today.

This group of song writers inspired Dorsey, who rhythmically stepped up the music by bringing to it more of the idioms that he had used as a blues pianist. (This writer, on more than one occasion, has heard Baptist choruses of five hundred or more led by Miss Campbell, Dorsey, and others sing this music.) Dorsey was joined by Theodore Frye, Kenneth Morris, Lillian Bowles, Sallie Martin, and Roberta Martin in bringing to the fore gospel music that was, in its early days, rejected by many serious black musicians. It caused protests in several Baptist churches and split several choirs. Ministers eager to attract the young and the unchurched organized new choirs, not to replace older ones, but to help in "firing" up the services.

In time, robes, stoles, and hoods of many and varied colors and fabrics began to be part of the dress of these new choirs and demonstrative actions often accompanied their renditions. And the emotional pitch must not be slighted. Without it the numbers fail, sometimes painfully. With it they rise to unbelievable heights. These songs have taken on length according to the way they are received. If an audience is really moved, one song might last fifteen minutes or more.

Compared to spirituals, the texts of "gospels" are weak, and audiences will not be able to join in readily since the performers are singing special arrangements. The accompaniments, which are essential, frequently call for piano, organ, guitar, and bass. But, we repeat, emotion is the core.

The sources of the texts are not very different from spiritual textual sources. An early "gospel" which begins, "I was young, but I recall singing songs was mother's joy," moves on to a couple with the hymn, "Amazin' Grace." A well-known recording by the Edwin Hawkins singers borrows a snatch from the old, white gospel hymn "O Happy Day," and "I Heard the Voice." Others are original in text but not in music. In fact, Dorsey's famous "Precious Lord" is a warmed-over version of "Must Jesus Bear the Cross Alone?" The text is new, but not the music. Let us hasten to explain that this is not intended to steal the compositions of others. As was the case in the era of the oral tradition, you were free to borrow as long as you made the borrowed music better than you found it. Everyone knows that written gospels are mere indications of what the composer intends; the performer is to make it better. If you have ever heard Mahalia Jackson sing Dorsey's "Precious Lord," you know that you certainly did not hear "Must Jesus Bear," you really heard "Precious Lord."

Today, gospel singers have taken the music into night club theaters, city auditoriums, Broadway productions, ("Don't Bother Me, I Can't Cope," "Black Nativity" "Your Arms Are Too Short to Box with God") jazz festivals, and into formerly conservative Methodist and Congregational churches.

Beginning at Howard University in 1970, gospel music "goes to college." Many colleges and universities began developing black choirs which made extensive use of gospel music. Some of these musical groups developed spontaneously out of the spiritual needs of collegians. Some were encouraged by black study programs or minority development offices. The music is not tied to academia but is a clear acknowledgement of the emotional and spiritual needs of developing youths. An annual meeting of these choirs (National Black Gospel College Choir Workshop) is held each year during the Thanksgiving or Christmas vacation periods. Since the mid-seventies, these have been held in Atlanta.

Gospel music in the 1970s has been given special popularity by James Cleveland, a former musician with Mahalia Jackson. Cleveland has extended his music through concerts, recordings, radio, television, and his Gospel Music Workshops that are held regularly across the country. Thousands learn his music, style, and participate in live recording sessions. This style and music are then transferred to local congregations. A prolific musician, Cleveland's influence is strong in black churches and with gospel music choirs in America, the Caribbean, and Africa.

As stated earlier, the music from the black church is a music that takes as its license the right to pick and choose that which serves its needs, and if it cannot be found, it may be created. The fact that it begins as outright creation makes creativity part and parcel of all black music, sacred as well as secular. The offerings are honest and they are intended to serve the human needs of the people, individual and group. As an honest music that without doubt has had many positive effects on those who use it, it should have been, at least at the level of the music of the oral tradition, accepted into the larger body of church music of the Christian world. It is the hope of this writer that church musicians will begin to integrate some of it into their music portions of the worship service.

Notes

1. Harold Courlander, *Negro Folk Music, U.S.A.* (New York: Columbia University Press, 1963), p. 39.

2. Dena J. Epstein, "Slave Music in the United States Before 1860: A Survey of Sources," in *Notes of the Music Library Association,* 20 (Spring and Summer 1963), pp. 195-212, 377-80.

3. James Weldon Johnson and J. Rosamond Johnson, *The Books of American Negro Spirituals* (New York: Viking Press, 1942), pp. 21-23.

4. Richard Allen, quoted in John Lovell, Jr., *Black Song: The Forge and the Flame* (New York: Macmillan & Co., 1972), pp. 105-106.

5. Daniel Alexander Payne, quoted in Eileen Southern, *Readings in Black American Music* (New York: W. W. Norton & Co., 1971), pp. 65-70.

6. Ibid., pp. 68-69.

7. Fredrika Bremer, *Homes of the New World,* n.p., n. d., pp. 107-108 and 112-113.

8. Joseph R. Washington, Jr., *Black Religion* (Boston: Beacon Press, 1964), p. 200.

9. Eileen Southern, *The Music of Black Americans: A History* (New York: W. W. Norton & Co., 1971), pp. 39-40.

10. John W. Work, "Plantation Meistersinger," *The Musical Quarterly,* 27; Jan. 1941, pp. 97-106.

11. Miles Mark Fisher, *Negro Slave Songs in the United States* (Ithaca, N.Y.: Cornell University Press, 1953), p. 25.

12. V. F. Calverton, "The Negro and American Culture," *Saturday Review of Literature,* 22, 21 Sept. 1940, p. 17*ff.*

13. John W. Work, "The Negro Spiritual," Paper No. 24, (New York: Hymn Society of America, 1961), pp. 17-27.

14. See J. B. Marsh, *The Story of the Jubilee Singers and Their Songs* (London: Hodder and Stoughton, 1875).

15. R. Nathaniel Dett, "Listen to the Lambs," (New York: G. Schirmer, Inc., 1914).

16. James Weldon Johnson and J. Rosamond Johnson, *The Books of American Negro Spirituals* (New York: Viking Press, 1942).

17. Work, *The Musical Quarterly,* p. 22

18. Pearl Williams-Jones, "Afro-American Gospel Music (1930-1970)," Howard University College of Fine Arts Project in African Music (Washington, D.C.). See also E. Franklin Frazier, *The Negro Church in America* (New York: Schoken Books, Inc., 1963).

19. See William J. Reynolds, *Songs of Our Faith* (Nashville: Broadman Press, 1964), pp. 423-424 for information about Tindley and a list of his gospel songs.

6
Black Preaching
Henry H. Mitchell

I begin by setting my topic in context. In other words, I must not attempt to write in a vacuum on the whole subject of black preaching. We must know how the subject relates to the white Southern Baptist preaching tradition and to the Christian tradition in general. Or at least we must understand how I *think* they are related—what are my own basic assumptions. This chapter will hinge on these, and whatever I say can be understood in their light.

Concerning white Southern Baptist preaching as related to black preaching, I share this experience. During the early 1940s some of my newfound Union Seminary schoolmates and I did a mental survey of the great preachers of New York City and Philadelphia. In our youthful but, as we thought of it, great wisdom, we decided that practically all of them came either from British possessions or from the American South. There was Buttrick from Scotland and Joseph Fort Newton from the South. So it went at length.

In due season we were moved to a consideration of why this was so. The guesses were many and varied. As I remember it, the two most impressive hypotheses were something like this: one had to do with poetry of the soul, a quality-employing language and rhetoric, but perhaps best described as an impressive fusion of beauty, spiritual sensitivity, and stimulating scholarship. It was a quality which we agreed was all too often squelched, if indeed it was ever born, in the industrial centers of the North.

106 Black Church Life-Styles

The other explanation was even harder to phrase—let's call it dramatic involvement. Other terms might include "less-inhibited expression" of the total person, "warmth" or "liberty in the spirit." Interestingly enough, this mostly white group of students seemed to think that this strength of Southern preaching may have stemmed from the large black presence and its influence on the culture of the South.

Whatever the validity of our impressions at that time, I have said all that to indicate that I have all these years held the clear assumption that Southern Baptist preaching has much more in common with American black preaching than any other white preaching in the United States. I also tend to feel that this is one of the reasons that the best-known revival preacher in America—Billy Graham—and many other pulpit powers are, in fact, Southern Baptists. I also have a long-standing conviction that *if* this power were to be focused, with all possible intensity and spiritual creativity, on the racial evils of the South and the nation, the South would easily assume the lead over the North in the whole field of brotherhood. In fact, I believe that for this and other reasons, the South could quite plausibly be the first area of our nation to solve outright the problems arising from centuries of white racial oppression and prejudice.

This reminds me of another incident which took place in the 1950s. I was serving as assistant to a white American Baptist executive whose original home had been Texas. I had heard that he had paid a visit to the Southern Baptist Convention headquarters in Nashville after attending an executive meeting in Saint Louis. In my typically frank way, I wanted to know what he was doing at "enemy" headquarters and at whose expense he went. The answer he gave, as we drove down the highway, will always ring in my soul. It was not long after the Supreme Court decision desegregating the schools, and he had gone to Nashville to try to convince some of his old friends in high office there of their strategic place in the spiritual history of the world. You see, he agreed with me that the greatest need in the Southern Baptist pulpit was a world-shaking goal like, maybe, brotherhood. He was also certain that if they would tackle it, the greatest revival in world history would break out. The irony of it was that many of the men he approached heartily agreed with him. They said, some with tears in their eyes, that they wished they had the faith to try, or they wished they had a greater sense that this was an idea whose time had come. My dear friend, the white executive originally from Texas, was surely not ahead of God's will, but he was far ahead of his fellow Southerners at the time.

The wisdom of this assertion is currently evident in some of the cities of the South where school integration has proceeded without incident and with much greater goodwill than in Boston or Chicago.

However, I am sure there can be no doubt, now, that the time has indeed come for all-out justice, brotherhood, and all that this may cost all of us in reordered priorities. And I suppose also that I have no right to hide my conviction that the best of Southern Baptist preaching could, with a proper acceptance of this mandate from heaven, set the South and the world on fire. I have this confidence partly because the best of Southern Baptist preaching is surely kin to the best of black preaching. They were born, for the most part, in the same place and at some of the same times, and they have lived side by side all these years. The black tradition went North and West sooner, but white Southerners have followed the same pattern of diaspora. The relationship between us, regardless of the horrible earlier history, is, in form and often in substance, the closest relationship we black preachers have outside the black world.

Black Preaching and the Total Christian Tradition

The relationship to the total Christian tradition is less known in depth, and much more subtle. Even to state the relationship, one has to establish first an understanding concerning basic Christianity as opposed to the widely prevalent, white Western version. Therefore I will briefly describe this contrast first.

The gospel was, as Paul said, foolishness (1 Cor. 1:23) to Greeks. It was not intellectually systematic. Today, we would say that it was "primitive." Paul was aware that this was no recommendation in Greek culture, and so he proceeded to remedy the erstwhile flaw, despite his protests to the contrary. He made his words to Greeks about Christ and the cross as cogent and systematic as possible. He moved so far in the direction of Greek culture as to quote a Stoic pantheist, thought by some to be Epimenides. He said, "For in him we live, and move, and have our being; as certain also of your own [Greek] poets have said" (Acts 17:28). He was *entering* their culture and building on their strengths. It never dawned on him to destroy or ignore so important a part of their lives. The result was that this Stoic pantheist quotation is now a part of our Holy Bible. And why not?

This inevitable and legitimate process of cultural entrance and adaptation was continued when Christianity was carried to northern Europe. This time it was so-called "pagan" festivals that were baptized into our faith, just as these Greek sayings and some other Greek religious practices had been baptized into the faith. The result was a Christianity now widely known for winter festivals with "Christmas trees," spring festivals with "Easter eggs," and a calendar with days like Sunday and Thursday, all of these clearly indicating "pagan" objects and styles of worship.

I have no quarrel with any of this. The problem is simply that when Christianity was carried to other continents, this same cultural adaptability ceased. Thus, European holidays, attire, language, and customs were declared to be *the* definitive "Christianity." *This was cultural imperialism and violence of the worst sort, and all over the world, people are more and more aware of it.* Not only did it destroy the people thus belittled, and not only did it destroy the full impact of Christ on them and their culture, it also impoverished the gospel itself by robbing it of the enrichment that has come every time the faith has had genuine dialogue with any culture. When Paul reached out toward the Greeks, he capitalized on their strengths and thus enriched Christianity as a *whole*. In so doing he helped to give the gospel the greatest adaptability, perhaps, of any world religion in the facing of the modern intellectual revolution, the age of science, and the cause-and-effect world view.

My quarrel is that there are other challenges to be faced by the gospel and other cultures with other strengths to be used of God in the facing of those problems. We *need* desperately, today, what God could do for all men through these cultures and their interpretation of His Word. But white arrogance has caused missionaries and others to assume that white Western culture, much like the Bible, was *the culture* once and for all delivered to the saints. I feel especially keen about this because black Christianity and black preaching have been considered outside the accepted and "orthodox" mainstream where God is at work in the world. Thus, when whites begin losing their young people and facing other weaknesses in their faith, they have carefully avoided black models in their search for answers. In the 1960s and early '70s they tried coffeehouses, guitars and drums, so-called "dialogue," and so-called "celebration." We've been doing this sort of thing for over two hundred years. But nobody seems willing to search all out for the ways in which such elements have been used in black religion, not as instant culture gimmicks but as time-honored aspects of a highly developed religion and culture.

I have real questions about people who go out and suddenly "make" a culture or a style of worship. These things have to come with long rootage in human experiences. If they want to dialogue with old roots, we've got them. If they want to know what celebration is all about, that's all we ever did. We did that before we heard about Jesus. Thus, despite the sometimes-close kinship, nobody has set out seriously to study the black pulpit for the saving inputs it might offer the white pulpit. It's fine for the best of black preachers to skim cream off the best of two worlds, but whites often seem determined to settle for the narrow impoverishment of only one culture. Encouragingly, some changes have occurred in several predominantly white seminaries which have, or are seeking, black professors of homiletics.

All of this is to say only two things about black Christianity and its relationship to Christianity: (1) Our black ancestors did in fact engage in their own independent adaptation of their African culture and traditional religions to Christianity. (2) The result has been a very powerful and relevant black Christianity, when seen at its best. Whatever blacks do that is different from what whites do—whatever we have kept of our African heritage—is *at least* as legitimate as Christmas trees and Easter eggs. It may have in some ways been even more faithful to the original primitive Christianity which was started as oral tradition in a culture quite similar to West African and several other so-called "primitive" cultures. The fact that it deals, therefore, with the still-primitive feelings of all people, while integrating into itself the wisdom of the intellectual revolution, makes black religion and especially black preaching at their best a very possibly chosen instrument or vessel of God for these perilous days. It would be difficult to conceal my conviction that this is so.

One other area of understanding must be established. It has to do with *which* of the many facets of black preaching I shall be thinking of when I use the term. First, let me repeat that I shall be thinking of the best—the most soundly biblical and practically relevant preaching—as well as the most inspired and creative. I seek models for inspiration and guidance, not targets for criticism. Let us consider the *successes* rather than the failures.

I also write primarily of that which reaches the vast majority of blacks. The wide spectrum of black preaching includes varying degrees of traditional African influence and modern American black rural and urban ghetto influence. But all of these varieties are one in their attempts to keep alive and to liberate an oppressed people. Formal education, social and economic status vary, however, causing variety in black preaching. Threads of the single experience run through them all, but if I seem to speak more of that variety which reaches the black masses, it may be because those threads are more obvious.

I make this statement because I want it understood that while there are other black folks besides Baptists, Pentecostals, and Methodists, I speak of them because this is where the typology shows itself more clearly. Some of my friends seem to think that I am trying to wish the black Presbyterians and Episcopalians out of business, but that just isn't so. I only want them to come home culturally. I don't care what denominational label they have; if they preach with the style and conviction of our black fathers, somebody will be saved.

A History of Black Religion

Let us now survey black preaching itself, much of which is contained in my book by the same name. As I talk about black preaching, I am aware of continuing resistance to the idea that we are different, but I am strongly inclined to believe we are and glad of it. We must then look for the historical roots of black preaching and black religion. This is necessary to legitimatize our faith and our utterance in the minds of a great many black militants—so-called—who insist on saying: "Black religion was something white folks gave us; a game they ran on us to make us docile and pliable, to make us good servants who would work hard with no complaints."

Let me say, first of all, that for the longest time white people *didn't want* us to become Christians. In fact, they didn't want to admit we had a soul. From 1619 when the first slaves landed until 1773 there was no black church anywhere, only blacks in white church galleries. For nearly two centuries afterward, blacks had no concentrated exposure to Christianity. During that period of time, all sorts of blacks became Christian, and very often because they *wanted to* and not because anybody was trying to teach them. To be sure, there were people who did teach. For example, at my wife's hometown in South Carolina the Episcopalians started out bright and early (1695) teaching us to read, so that we could study the catechism and use the prayer book. Some of the most dangerous people, from the white view of their ability to lead blacks, came out of South Carolina because they taught us "rascals" to read "too quick." South Carolina continued even through 1920 to be the "capital" of black intellectual production for church leaders, perhaps for this reason.

Apart from these few exceptions, the vast majority of blacks had to "steal" their Christian faith by listening to what was said to others. In the process they only slowly came to be what we now know as Christians, but they were still *often* ahead of their masters. This accounts for men like Richard Allen, who was said to have led his master to conversion, and not vice versa.

In that period they picked up bits and snatches which meshed with their original African traditional religion. In other words, nobody had to sell them a bill of goods. Nobody had to press them. The religion they had when they came here was quite compatible with Christianity. Since they were from many African languages they had to talk about their religion in English, which means that their faith had a Christian set of terms very likely before they had a legitimate standing in what we call orthodox Christian religion.

Miles Mark Fisher, in his *Negro Slave Songs in the United States,* quoted a report written in the nineteenth century on a camp meeting where a black brother was preaching to some of his folk. He had on a strange set of clothes, which was quite typical because blacks always believed when you were going to religious observance you ought to have the "best" of everything. So if the preacher had on a full-dress formal with tails flying, that was what he believed he was supposed to be wearing according to his African understanding of worship.

The report goes on to say that the gestures, the sounds, and the words he was saying were "a very strange way to address the Deity." Whether whites understood him or not, it is undeniable that over the seventeenth and eighteenth centuries blacks were gradually shaping their own Christianity and using it in ways familiar to them. When they finally became what we would call thoroughbred "orthodox"

Black Preaching

Christians, they still had a great deal of the styles, movements, and expressions of their original African traditional religion. Some of the things we call "country" and "ignorant"—some of the things that happened in cotton-patch churches—are in fact direct descendants of the worship you can still see in traditional religion in Africa today.

I have had Africans tell me that when they came to the United States and sat in a black Baptist church, the words were different, the songs were different, but the movements and all sorts of other things were the same as traditional (non-Christian) worship. Though they didn't understand what was going on, they felt very much at home. Having been in traditional worship in Africa, I can say the same thing. There is such a remarkable kinship between traditional African religion and what we practice today that whatever is really rich about black religion, compared with white religion, is the *African* component. This is comparable to the enrichment of Christianity which Paul gave when he tried to adjust it to the *Greek* culture.

When we are different, therefore, let it be understood that we have good reason for being so, and what we have that is different must not be destroyed. We must quit deciding that going to seminary is to change us to sound like white folks. My position—my job as a black church studies professor (and primarily black seminary dean)—is to make sure we do not lose these characteristics. Now I'll wax intellectual in my classes and talk about all of those big theological terms. But I want to be sure that when those fellows go out with all of those terms in the back of their heads, and when they get ready to talk to "Aunt Jane," they will not be speaking a foreign language.

I am thoroughly convinced that what happened to our forefathers is that they were acculturated in some way to pick the best of two worlds. But when people talk of an absolutely "converted" African, I question this. They already had such strong characters, such unselfish values. They had all sorts of things that were so completely Christian that missionaries in many cases have sold us a terrible bill of goods when they talked about those "pagans" bowing down to wood and stone.

I was doing some research in 1971 and collaborated with a lady who went out in the streets to interview people. She found person after person from traditional villages who could quote more Bible and more African proverbs, which often sounded the same, than you will find from anybody here who has been through all of the American Sunday Schools. And it is so deeply ingrained in the culture that they don't know *when* they learned it.

African traditional religion and African culture are very strong. There is no problem in preparing for Christian faith, for even Jesus is prepared for by a great deal of what they believe.

Having said all of this, I agree with many scholars who now believe that what happened during the "hidden years" (1623-1775) is what I refer to in my book as the emergence of the "black fathers." Their Christianity was now accepted, or black Christianity was "adequately Christian" or "legitimate." They had all of these years been developing the *fusion* between African religion, culture, and Christianity. What they did at that point began immediately to be seen as a tremendously powerful, black Christian witness.

One can read the writings of a British traveler by the name of Charles Lyell who attended a service where Andrew Marshall was preaching in the First African Baptist Church in Savannah. Marshall became pastor of that church in 1812. This Britisher wrote, in effect: "I never dreamed I'd find such worship among Blacks." This, incidentally, can be found in a documentary history of blacks that has been published by two men named Fishel and Quarles. The British traveler said this church had a huge congregation. The pastor preached a very, very intelligent sermon on "The Eagle Stirs Her Nest." He said "the man used the animals [as African culture does], to teach many lessons." It is very likely that he picked the eagle out of the Bible because Africans talk about birds and animals to tell their children all of the lessons they need to know. When he "lapsed" into black English, into their dialect, it was very obvious that he was doing so to increase the impact of his point, and not because he suddenly waxed "ignorant" and "went to speaking" the black folks' language.

All of this seems clearly to document that at the beginning of the nineteenth century this fusion had already taken place, to the extent that all over the colonies where black people were, there was this same kind of powerful utterance which people without any training were guided and blessed by God to develop. When I say "without any training," I guess I should reverse that and acknowledge what is really the learning process. I have already done this and indicated it in my book *Black Preaching*.

Training of the Black Preacher

This same pastor Andrew Marshall did, in fact, have opportunities for learning. His use of language indicates the white part, and his handling of the eagle narrative indicates the African or black part. He and his successors did receive a form of "training," and the way the church reports it in its own documentary history is almost by accident. They were bragging about the effect of the first pastor having been a "body servant." This means that he was not a field hand, but was in the house and was constantly exposed to "standard" English language, reading, writing, and so forth. Thus, he became fluent and was, on the basis of this educational process, able to lead a great church. Andrew Marshall, the second pastor, went a little further in his exposure. The process for each pastor moves on further, so the last "untrained" pastor in terms of formal education was a man who had been a body servant and had *gone to Europe* with his master. These leaders were determined to learn and to pick up the technicalities of white culture so they could go back and lead their folk. Here was a man who had been to Europe as a servant and was a great leader on the basis of this kind of education, coupled with his black understanding.

Their first formally educated pastor was a man who finished Morehouse College. He came in 1885, having finished in one of the earlier classes. I think of my own home-church pastor (obviously before my time), a man by the name of Poindexter, about whom Carter Woodson, the black historian, wrote a great deal. Poindexter got his education as a *barber,* across the street from the statehouse at Columbus, Ohio. He was pastor of the Second Baptist Church for some forty years. He held high political (elected) office. He was obviously a very intelligent, first-rate leader. But the education that he received was while people thought he was cutting their hair, but he was actually "picking their brains."

When we look at the "black fathers," we are *compelled* to ask: "How did they become so sharp?" How could they do the tremendous work they did during the reconstruction when black preachers launched black businesses, black education, black churches, stabilized black families, and did a fantastic piece of work in government? The Golden Age of the black church was the reconstruction period, and it was the golden age because of the tremendous heights to which black preachers rose both as preachers and as leaders.

When you look at all of this and wonder how, the only explanation is that they went to and fro upon the earth picking up what they could find everywhere they could find it. Even though I am a professor in a well-known seminary, I suspect that a person who would be willing, as methodically as those men did, to study everything he saw, could become just as educated as they did.

However, the fact of our time is that people who don't go to school to get what they need usually won't get it anywhere else either. So I have to suggest that most of the people go on to accredited schools today.

When I talk about the "black fathers," the great preachers, I am talking about men who learned what they did—about the Bible and about life and about all the various disciplines which men like Poindexter acquired—by listening to everything they heard, finding what they could find, and putting it together. That sort of thing may culminate in a kind of evolution in succeeding generations. Martin Luther King, Jr., had all of the college degrees including the Ph.D., but he kept the same kind of style and culture orientation that his preacher-father and grandfather had had. His power did not arise from his education in white schools, but despite his education, because he stood solidly in the tradition of his "black fathers," holding on to the best of their African heritage, culling the best of the white heritage, and fusing them to develop what we know as the black pulpit.

Beliefs of Black Preachers

Now I must tell what these men believed by way of expression. Blacks took the Bible very seriously, and for reasons easily traceable to their African roots. In their African roots they had known huge quantities of memorized material. Even now the history, which is still more sung than written, is known by anybody. In one of the festivals, if the performer makes one mistake, 200 people will say, "Whoa, go back." I mention this because, though many of these men were "illiterate," they came out of where people (Ife priests) *memorized* thousands of proverbs. (Alex Haley's book *Roots* has since widely publicized these oral historians called "griots.")

In the Yoruba religion they have sixteen odus. Each odu has two-hundred proverbs or stories, so some of those Yoruba priests may know about as much verbatim as we have in the whole Bible. When you go to them for leadership, guidance, or divination, these men call it right up. This explains to a large extent the way in which blacks have adapted themselves to the Bible. The Bible largely reflected the kind of culture out of which they came. The Old Testament was so much like their culture, with veneration for their fathers, and so forth, that some of the white missionaries hid the Old Testament. Had they shown those fellows the Old Testament, they would have said: "So what's new? Who needs it? We've got that already."

The Bible in the American black tradition quickly grew to huge importance and achieved the same kind of standing in their thinking that the old African proverbs had done. While you may say, "They were two, three, or four generations removed from that," the fact is that all of this cultural orientation continued. The *only* way you wipe out the culture, the world view, or any other view that goes with it is to wipe out *people.*

Those who maintain the idea that blacks lost their culture may be right when they talk about some minor things, but in the important things like religion, we've kept a whole lot more than most people think. (Note: The veneration of age in African and Old Testament culture is alive and well in the black church. The importance of a water rite called baptism is old-hat African. So is the sense of church as extended family, and so is the shouting, though assigned a different significance.)

We see this when we look at the way blacks use the Bible. They revere the Bible, but not in the rigid, print-bound, Western sense. Their proverbs and their holy writings, or whatever you wish to call them, were used much more dynamically than the literalism that prevails among many others who take the Bible "seriously."

Blacks have kept all of the strengths of the so-called primitive approach to the Bible, at the same time absorbing and integrating the intellectual world view we now have, without letting it kill the religion. So blacks are not generally literalistic.

The result has been that the average black audience would not listen to a preacher for five minutes if he didn't take a text. I know many people preach textless now, and they tell us at some seminaries that we don't necessarily have to have a text. Maybe that is so with some folk, but "Man, don't you be going to no black church talkin' 'bout 'my topic' " with no text.

This is a tremendous strength. It is one of the things that has made the black pulpit and church as strong as it is today. The kinds of doctrinal positions that the Bible suggests, again, have been taken very seriously, but not with the rigidity that makes people go to extremes like they call them in the intellectual world, *reductio ad absurdum.*

Black Preaching

We don't just take an idea and force it to the point where it is completely out of touch with reality.

The black pulpit has been much more concerned therefore with experience and relevance. The black preacher preaches to a point, and he is very willing, as were Martin Luther King and all of his forebears, to deal with politics and any other thing that had to be dealt with. They are fully aware that all just concerns are a part of the very will of God and His kingdom. While the black preacher is a Bible-centered preacher, he is also a very life-oriented preacher.

This kind of a stance has kept the black pulpit very lively. I can still take you to places where people come early, hoping to get a seat in a three-thousand-seat auditorium, because somebody is proclaiming the Word in the same tradition of the "black fathers."

Let me say one other thing about the intellectual and doctrinal stance of the black pulpit. The black pulpit has not been hobbled by this whole crisis between science and reason on the one hand, and faith on the other. The black pulpit in its concern for life takes the supernatural very much in stride. We believe in folks getting healed. Blacks include healing of the mind, body, and soul in their traditional religion. This is not amiss, as Dr. T. E. Lambo, the head of a section of the World Health Organization, affirms the relationship between the health of the soul and mind and that of the body. Lambo indicates that the psychiatric effectiveness of traditional religion at many points has been better than that of his clinical staff of psychiatrists in Western Nigeria.

I am not trying to do away with the use of psychiatrists. I am only saying that the supernatural is very real in the black pulpit. It has not succumbed to the idea that we have to know all of the *causes* for everything. If that were the case, we would have to do away with life, for we still don't know how it is caused—if we do away with the idea of God as Creator of life and the universe. In a word, the black church is quite comfortable in a world where everything is subject to the sovereignty of God.

Black Preaching Style

Now consider style in the black pulpit. This is one of the more crucial issues once one has looked at this historical and doctrinal base of the black pulpit. Style has to do with the kind of colorful utterance, mannerisms, and so forth that we have come to associate with the black pulpit.

The first aspect has to do with stylistic freedom. The black pulpit has assumed a certain openness and permissiveness that makes it possible for a person to do almost anything he wants to if he does it sincerely. Some of you may know my dear friend who pops his suspenders. Some of you knew another man who said, "Bless my bones" (the late T. M. Chambers, Sr.), and all of this. Nobody worries about these things because they are a part of each one's flavor as a person. These men did not go somewhere and get told that they had to stick their fingers up at a particular time and raise their voices at a certain point. They do it *their* way and let *God* use them.

While there is a sense in which this occurs in other traditions, there is no doubt that the colorfulness of the black pulpit is one of the reasons why people still go long distances to hear the black preacher preach. This is also symbolically important because black people live in a world where there is not much freedom. Even today, there is far less freedom than the average white mind can even imagine. On some occasions when white friends have been rather fully exposed to how completely limited the black world is, it has brought them to the verge of a nervous breakdown. The guilt feelings can be so bad that many white folks ought not to know how bad it really is because they might not be able to take it.

The black pulpit is symbolically a place where people burst out of the bonds that have shackled them all week and are *literally free.* These *worshipers share vicariously* in the freedom of the preacher, to the extent that he does just what he feels like doing. They enjoy this.

I have a suspicion that other preachers could share this freedom if they could buck the tradition of detailed planning in worship. The average liturgical church follows that tradition right straight down the line. Everything has to conform. When you want to prove to people that you are very intelligent and educated, you follow those forms. Then, of course, you are safe. The black preacher has to be willing to take the risks to be what he is and assume that God will use it in a way that is creditable both to the Kingdom enterprise and to the preacher. It's a harder way but much better. The freedom in the pulpit is symbolic of the freedom all people must have, and it is much more effective in the way it speaks to the condition of people.

One of the more technical aspects of black preaching is the whole language which is used. I asked a friend of mine to write the foreword for my book on *Black Preaching*. He finally decided that he couldn't do it because he couldn't take the chapter on black language. The reason for this was very simple. He opposed a reality: language is a status signal. He didn't like the idea that when people talk to us, they ought to sound the way *we* sound. I suppose the most profound thing that was said in the whole book was that when we quote God we ought to quote Him in the native tongue. Language is a symbol. It is a sign. It tells people who we are.

Now, I don't *look* very black. Sometimes people say, "O Lord! Here's a white man. I *know* he can't preach." But the minute "Ah gits up and starts to talking" (extreme to dramatize a point), the atmosphere changes. Some people come afterwards to say, "When I saw you up in the pulpit, I said, 'O Lord! We ain't goin' to get a drop this morning.' But the minute you opened your mouth, I knowed who you was." Why, you see, that's just what I *wanted* them to know. The sound image takes precedence over the visual image. Anytime we can *sound* like folk, we can reach them regardless of what we *look* like.If I am quoting God, I don't want Him to sound like some distant alien. Just as *visual* images must conform to the people, to diminish the distance between those people and their God, so must the *ear* images conform. People must hear God in speech that contrasts with their speech so little that the feel: "He's one of us." I have on many occasions carefully prearranged to speak the words of God, not in the so-called proper, "standard" dialect of the middle-class white, to indicate that God is one of *us*. For example, when I speak about Peter in the vision where God told him, "Rise, Peter; kill, and eat" (Acts 10:13). and Peter said, "What? Lord, I've *never* let anything like that touch *my* lips, *nothin'* common and dirty" (author's paraphrase). Instead of having God speak in the "proper" white dialect, I say, "Looka here, Peter, don't you call nothin' *Ah* made unclean." This is the way a man would say it in black English.

If we want God to be real to black people, linguistics must also be used to present a picture of God to whom they can relate. We are not yet in a world where people are linguistically any one thing. There is no universal culture or language, and until the cultures fuse, we must keep religion in the language we use. When the economic, educational, and other experiences have leveled out, the cultures *will* fuse. One reason we have a different culture now is that we have a poorer "break," a different experience. Until the experiences level out, justice prevails, and people forget color, there will be no forgetting culture. This culture will be perpetuated as long as the differences are as arbitrarily established and enforced as they are. This is why black language becomes an important part of black preaching, especially to the black masses.

Black preaching also uses a lot of imagination. The culture of West Africa is full of stories, engaging stories, some sung, some told. The history of the black pulpit is a history of utterance that has been highly conditioned by the same kind of storytelling tradition. Thus when a black preacher gets up and says, "I saw John on the Isle of Patmos early one Sunday morning," he is putting into details that which implies: "I was an eyewitness. As an eyewitness I give you a living account." Then he gives a living account that people can relate to.

I taught a course once at a Rochester Catholic seminary called "The Black Bible and Black Imagination." The whole purpose of the course was to teach Roman Catholic priesthood candidates how to tell the Bible story, so it would live a little bit. I had an interesting experience when one of the students came back. It reminded me of the time when the disciples came back and told Jesus, "Even the devils are subject unto us" (Luke 10:17). (They were surprised because, even though Jesus had told them how to do it, they didn't expect victories; so their return was with joy and surprise.) This young, Italian-American fellow came back to class, and he said, "Great experience, but I had one problem. I got into the story, and those people were really responding; I got carried away, and I took *seventeen* minutes. I wasn't supposed to take but ten. It made the mass go seven minutes late. This meant that all of the cars for the next mass were strung up and down the street because they couldn't get into the parking lot—all because I was telling that story." I told him that since this was such a dangerous device, he ought to save it for the last mass when no one else was coming after.

This gift of black Bible storytelling is the same kind of thing that we get in the Joel Chandler Harris version of Br'er Rabbit. Harris only sat down and wrote what he heard black folk saying. He didn't *create* anything. He was only a reporter. The kinds of detail, the kinds of humor, the kinds of pointed utterance we associate with the black imagination in the pulpit are very important. People even today, regardless of color, will listen to a black Bible story and never get tired.

At Princeton Seminary, I did a three-lecture series on the black Bible. At the end I gave the students the option of calling out a story so I could "blackenize" it on the spot. They were delighted and, I think, fed. They would have kept me up there all day. They were not at all anxious to leave. When they asked for Ezekiel's dry bones, I just climaxed with that one and sat down on my own, over their protest. This is the sort of thing the whole world needs. The black preacher must not lose his touch at doing it.

The Future of Black Preaching

Just a few words now on the future of black preaching. At this moment black preaching is in the beginning of a major renaissance. That which we are trying to do at our seminary is paralleled in many of the major schools across our nation. Instead of sending men out for the "best" seminaries to sound "white" and flunk out in the black pulpit, we are sending them out to preach in the "mother tongue" to ordinary folk. We have student preachers who have the best of everything. Some can translate Paul Tillich's ideas into biblical "blackese" and preach them with power. Some can correlate this with the Bible and cause people to learn things they never would have known otherwise. These fellows are quite relevant; they know what black folk need and how to give it to them. They can be most effective because no one else in the black community can come near the black pulpit in terms of influence and effect. You can be sure that these fellows will be using that influence for any necessary activities related to the kingdom of God.

In addition to the renaissance in curriculum, the seminaries are recruiting young blacks as never before, even in Southern Baptist seminaries. At one time, my seminary never had more than four black students. Today we have forty. We have more than any nonblack seminary in the nation and more than all black seminaries except one. We have six full-time black faculty members, but we are still out beating the bushes and recruiting young blacks for ministerial preparation. A great many of these people will go out bivocationally qualified. Some will have degrees in social service, law, or business. They will be able to take churches that never really had skilled leadership and lead them to Kingdom greatness while still practicing their second professions. *(Editor's Note:* This was written when the author was at the Colgate-Rochester Divinity School in 1971. Currently, he is dean of the School of Theology at Virginia Union University, and ninety of his 101 students are black.)

If this present trend continues, I see in the future of the black church a tremendous growth in the pulpit. It is also true that our accomplishments are getting much better coverage than they once did. A fellow like Jesse Jackson, whose whole base of operation is built on his preaching—as little as some people might realize it—is the sort of person who causes young men to say, "You know if I could do that, I might let the Lord call me."

The preaching ministry is no longer a thing to be done only when you can't pass medical school tests. We will continue to draw more and more seminary students and provide better and more relevant training. For this I thank God and look with great joy to the future.

One other thing I would like to suggest is that whatever we do in the seminaries is bound to influence the white student as well as the black. I took part in a workshop this year combining the black and white preaching labs. By far, the more eager students who wanted to come in and go over their outlines before they preached them, who sat and listened to every pearl on black preaching, were the white students.

We have quite a mixture at our seminary. There are the High Church Episcopalians who have Eucharist a couple of days a week. Then we have just regular white Protestant services a couple of times a week. On Wednesday, we have "high holy day." That's the day we "have church." There are more people who come to "church" on Wednesday than any of the other services. I should have pointed this out earlier: while I said that whites have scrupulously avoided looking at blacks as models for anything, on the seminary campus today a great many whites are beginning to recognize the tremendous power of the black church and the black pulpit.

The Episcopalians are really taking this very seriously. Dr. Gardner Taylor had six white Episcopalians in one course several years ago. He happens to teach at our school, in addition to the six full-time black men. With this happening, it is quite conceivable that some white Protestant churches, which in some instances are in death throes statistically, may yet be brought back to life. The black church may offer the saving possibility to other racial church traditions as well.

7
The Black Church's Outreach
W. J. Hodge

How shall we sing the Lord's song in a strange land? If I forget thee, O Jerusalem, let my right hand forget her cunning. If I do not remember thee, let my tongue cleave to the roof of my mouth; if I prefer not Jerusalem above my chief joy (Ps. 137:4-6).

Now when Ebed-melech the Ethiopian, one of the eunuchs which was in the king's house, heard that they had put Jeremiah in the dungeon; the king then sitting in the gate of Benjamin; Ebed-melech went forth out of the king's house, and spake to the king, saying, My lord the king, these men have done evil in all that they have done to Jeremiah the prophet, whom they have cast into the dungeon; and he is like to die for hunger in the place where he is: for there is no more bread in the city. Then the king commanded Ebed-melech the Ethiopian, saying, Take from hence thirty men with thee, and take up Jeremiah the prophet out of the dungeon, before he die. So Ebed-melech took the men with him, and went into the house of the king under the treasury, and took thence old cast clouts and old rotten rags, and let them down by cords into the dungeon to Jeremiah. And Ebed-melech the Ethiopian said unto Jeremiah, Put now these old cast clouts and rotten rags under thine armholes under the cords. And Jeremiah did so. So they drew up Jeremiah with cords, and took him up out of the dungeon: and Jeremiah remained in the court of the prison (Jer. 38:7-13).

The Spirit of the Lord is upon me, because he hath anointed me to preach the gospel to the poor; he hath sent me to heal the brokenhearted, to preach deliverance to the captives, and recovering of sight to the blind, to set at liberty them that are bruised, To preach the acceptable year of the Lord (Luke 4:18-19).

One of the strange, weird, perplexing, and paradoxical miracles of history is the origin of the black church on the North American continent. The dehumanizing, brutal, and barbaric fashion in which blacks were captured, shipped, and subsequently treated in the New World would seem to mitigate forever against their acceptance of the religion many of their masters were supposed to have had. If Cowper's famous "God moves in a mysterious way, His wonders to perform" needed any historical validation, the black church is it.

Anyone who reads a history of the black church will discover that its very origin was akin to the movement of the Christian faith beyond the narrow confines of Judaism in the first century. In that historic conference in Jerusalem as recorded in Acts 15, Simon Peter posed a question which found relevance in the first days of black Baptists and Methodists. Peter asked: "Now therefore why tempt ye God, to put a yoke upon the neck of the disciples, which neither our fathers nor we were able to bear?" (v. 10).

When Andrew Bryan was ordained on January 20, 1788, recognized, and invested with full authority to preach the gospel and to administer the ordinances of a Baptist church, there was a simultaneous fear that Bryan's work would only result in that of "servile insurrection." Slaves were arrested and severely punished for attending the meetings of this black Baptist preacher's church. Carter G. Woodson records that "Andrew Bryan and his brother Sampson, a deacon, were inhumanely cut and their backs were so lacerated that their blood ran down to the earth as they, with uplifted hands, cried to the Lord; but Bryan in the midst of his torture declared that he rejoiced not only to be whipped but would freely suffer death for the cause of Jesus Christ."[1] The courage of Andrew and Sampson Bryan reminds us of Peter and John as recorded in Acts 4.

The origin of African Methodists is no less heroic. Pulled from their knees as they prayed in a white Methodist church, Richard Allen, Absalom Jones, and William White led a group of black worshipers out of the Methodist church, which was to culminate in the organization of the African Methodist Episcopal Church in 1816.

In 1821, another step of secession from white-dominated Methodism was taken by black members of the Johns Street Methodist Episcopal Church in New York City. This led to the organization of the African Methodist Episcopal Zion Church.

African Methodism came into being because of an insatiable desire for independence. At first they had white Methodist preachers with local preachers of color serving under them. They notified the white Methodists that they no longer felt themselves obligated to look to them for supplying the pulpit.

It is not my purpose to do an exhaustive statement on the history of the black church. These three instances or origins, one in the South, two in the North, as well as subsequent origins of Baptist associations and conventions, dramatize and authenticate the assertion that the very origin of the black church was a movement of liberation and quasi-black religious nationalism. Blacks were in a strange, alien land, and having no African Jerusalem for which their hearts yearned, they did sing the Lord's song by the waters of the Mississippi.

It has been asserted that the black church has been an "opiate" for black people, dulling their senses to their miserable plight on earth. Joseph R. Washington, Jr., in his *Black Religion,* said, "Virtually from the beginning Negroes were introduced to the rewards of Christianity for the good of the planters in this world and for the good of the slaves in the world beyond."

Considering the brutality, the dehumanization, the satanic evil of slavery; the debauchery of Reconstruction with the development of a system of politics fashioned on grandfather clauses, poll taxes, and white primaries; inane legal definitions of "Negroes"; the development of a system of education designed to perpetuate the evil myth of white racial superiority, black inferiority, and a degrading isolation from the avenues of entrance into the American system; the development of an economic system based on: the resurrection of the old plantation, ill-gotten gains hatched out of the sharecropper bag, mere survival by menial labor, servitude by being domestics who found pieces of money "lost" by "Miss Jane" to encourage stealing, thus trying them with an iniquitous bond of loyalty—if the black church did no more than help us survive these by promises of a better world beyond, it is no less valid than the vision of John in Revelation during the Neronian and Diocletian persecutions.

The paradox is that though black preaching and worship were so conceived by white America, they stood in fear of the rise of the black church. In 1800 Gabriel Prosser, a slave, planned a revolt in Richmond, Virginia, which was betrayed by two slaves. Prosser used the "Bible to describe how slaves could assume the posture of the Israelites and discharge the bonds of slavery with the aid and comfort of God."[2]

In 1822 Denmark Vesey led an uprising in Charleston, South Carolina. According to Washington, members of the Negro Methodist Church were involved.

In 1831 Nat Turner led a bloody revolt at Southhampton County, Virginia. Nat Turner was a Baptist exhorter and mystic. It is said that he spent months in prayer and Bible reading before he even planned the insurrection.

Any good history book on the South will validate the assertion about fear. In 1833, Alabama made it unlawful for slaves or free Negroes to preach unless before respectable slaveholders and when authorized by some neighboring religious society. In 1834, Georgia enacted a law providing that neither free Negroes nor slaves might preach or exhort an assembly of more than seven unless licensed by justices on the certification of three ordained ministers. Other Southern states soon followed these examples, passing more drastic laws prohibiting the assembly of Negroes after the early hours of the night,

The Black Church's Outreach

and providing for the expulsion of all free Negroes from such commonwealths so as to reduce the danger of mischief and the spread of information by this more enlightened class. In *From Slavery to Freedom,* John Hope Franklin said that between 1830 and 1835 most states had outlawed Negro preachers.

My contention is that *the black church's outreach has always extended beyond the bounds of correct doctrine, Bible teaching, and Sunday meetings.* When you talk about the black people's God in His most authentic expression, He has always been a God of liberation, to set the captives free.

Equally as miraculous as its origin, has been the outreach of the black church. Among many other sources, one has only to read Frazier's *The Negro Church in America* to see the obstacles which had to be overcome.

1. There was, first of all, the damage done in the selling, buying, and transporting of slaves from Africa. They were bought for beads and rum. According to Frazier

> they were held in baracoons, a euphemistic term for concentration camps at the time, where slaves, without any regard for sex, or family and tribal affiliation were kept until some slaver came along to buy a cargo for the markets of the New World. In the Caribbean islands baracoons were also re-culturalization centers to docilize the slaves. This period of dehumanization was followed by the 'middle passage,' the voyage across the Atlantic Ocean to the slave markets of the West Indies and finally the indigo, tobacco, and cotton plantations of what was to become the United States of America. During the 'middle passage,' Negroes were packed "spoon-fashion" in the slave ships where no regard was shown for sex or age differences.[3]

2. The second barrier to the development of "peoplehood" was the size of the plantation and their orientation into their new university of Christian slavery. The majority of slaves were on small farms and small plantations. Thus, contact was minimized.

It is reported that new slaves were gradually regimented to work. They were made to bathe often, to take long walks, and especially to dance. They were distributed in small numbers among old slaves in order to better dispose them to acquire old-slave habits.

3. They were prohibited from preserving or using their own language. This was done in order to better cut off their lines of communication.

4. The plantation system was specifically designed to loosen all social bonds among them and to destroy their traditional basis of social cohesion.

5. The mobility of the slave system was highly prohibitive of any cohesion as well as a concept of a black slave by a white owner. Bancroft, in his *Slave Trading in the Old South,* quoted from *The Charleston Mercury* which stated, "Slaves are as much and as frequently articles of commerce as the sugar and molasses which they produce."[4]

6. The American slave system made insecure and precarious the most elementary form of social life, the family. There was no legal marriage. All relationships were temporary, dependent upon the will of the white masters and the exigencies of the plantation regime.

Sheares and others, in the November 2-16, 1970, issue of *Christianity and Crisis,* pointed out additional barriers imposed by the white church itself:

1. The exclusion of blacks from the ethical and moral protection of the church.

2. Provision of divine sanction and reinforcement for the system of slavery.

3. The incorporation into its own life and practices the separatist ways of society, the establishment of "nigger balconies," and the denial of "equal accommodations" and equal access to the ministerial services and resources of the church. "Negro pews" were often painted black, a derogatory sign in those days. Frequently blacks were not allowed to enter the church at all; they listened through open doors

and windows. Whites refused to share the Lord's Supper with them. Slaves took the Lord's Supper in the church basement or after the whites had gone home.

Despite these and other restrictions such as fugitive slave laws, laws of illegal assembly, the lack of formal education, little or no money, repression of expression, the preaching of an illegitimate theology, the black church developed and stretched forth its wings. The outlawing of black preachers and assembly without the presence of five whites, was a tacit admission of the recognition of the explosive, revolutionary power of the gospel of Jesus Christ by the white power structure of that day. Somehow, by God's grace working through the black slaves and some liberated, white Christians, the slaves discovered the explosive power of this gospel and stretched forth their wings to the Great Commission.

Educational Outreach

These so-called unlearned, unlettered, nonhuman beings developed schools to teach themselves and their offspring. George Lyle, a black Baptist preacher, organized and taught in a free school. Henry Adams, the first pastor of Fifth Street Baptist Church, Louisville, Kentucky, organized the first school for blacks in that city.

African Methodists founded such schools as: Wilberforce in Ohio, 1856; Allen University in South Carolina, 1881; Morris Brown, Atlanta, Georgia, 1885; Livingston College, North Carolina, 1889; and Lane College, Tennessee, 1889.

Black Baptists founded and organized such schools as: Selma University, Alabama, 1879; Arkansas Baptist College, Arkansas, 1884; State University, Louisville, Kentucky, 1873; Guadalupe College, Sequin, Texas, 1885; Virginia Theological Seminary, Lynchburg, Virginia, 1891; Friendship College, Rock Hill, South Carolina, 1891; Woman's National Training School, Washington, DC, 1909; and Morris College, Sumter, South Carolina.

There were other schools, of course, founded and operated for

134 Black Church Life-Styles

blacks by the American Baptist Home Mission Society. Such schools as Benedict College, South Carolina; Bishop College, now in Dallas; Shaw University, North Carolina; Spellman Seminary (for girls); Virginia Union University; Roger Williams University, which burned in 1905 and was reorganized under the control of Negro Baptists in Tennessee.

In 1947 the late Carter G. Woodson, black historian par excellence, had this to say of the black church:

> The Negro Church, handicapped as it has been, has accomplished some things impossible. In spite of the increasing influence of the public schools with largely augmented resources the church schools have continued and in poverty have produced the outstanding men of the race. (This is reminiscent of the Master's message to the church of Smyrna in Revelation—'I know thy works, and tribulation, and poverty—but thou art rich.') With their limited resources these church schools report a larger number of influential ministers than those richly endowed.[5]

Outreach in Significant Generalities

In 1945, Carter Woodson made the bold claim that "most movements among Negroes owe their success to the leadership of Negroes prominent in the Church." W. R. Pettiford, a preacher in Alabama, became one of the pioneer black bankers. This is also true of the late Henry Boyd and many others.

The black church has served as a newspaper, a forum for black expression, a school for the development of orators who have impressed the world as inspired spokespersons of a persecuted people. For many decades it was the only welfare agency we had. Even now, in crisis situations, it serves this purpose.

Wherever you find a black-owned and operated hospital, the church was a source of inspiration, funds, and public relations. Rural areas, small towns, and big cities formed burial and benevolent societies, credit unions, and insurance companies.

From my own small-town, rural background, I know that the church gave support to young physicians, morticians, teachers, and small businessmen.

In earlier years, many blacks regularly attended church whether Christian or sinners. Barred from other social centers, they went to church to see their friends. Having no automobiles, parks, or theaters, a young man went to church to meet his sweetheart, to impress her with his worth, and to woo her in marriage. The church was the school of agriculture for many farmers who had to depend upon the black farm agent for new information on growing crops or the reception of new government regulations. There was a time when, almost literally, the church was our "all and all."

The Black Church and the Freedom Movement

I go back to the freedom—civil rights—liberation movement because of the avalanche of criticism about the irrelevancy and impotence of the black church. If I were to say that the black church has lived up to its calling, I would be reckless with the truth. Nobody is more painfully aware of the shortcomings of the black church than the black preacher. But to say that it never has been and is not now a significant part of this movement is to ignore the truth.

The black church has always been possessed by a significant degree of radicalism and militancy. On September 15, 1830, black delegates met in the Bethel Church in Philadelphia to launch a series of conventions aimed at freedom. They advised some brothers to go to Canada. They condemned the American Colonization Society. They deprecated segregation as unjust, oppressive, and unconstitutional. They stressed the importance of education, temperance, and economy. Believe it or not, they set aside the Fourth of July as a day of "humiliation, fasting, and prayer" when blacks would ask for divine intervention to break the shackles of slavery.

We are all familiar with the rise of Martin L. King, Jr., and the Southern Christian Leadership Conference. Now as then, its leadership, base, and backbone was the black church. Martin Luther King talked about the power of nonviolence as Gandhi taught it, but when people marched, protested, demonstrated, and held their freedom rallies, it was always to the words and rhythm of the black spiritual.

One of the most creative aspects of SCLC was "Breadbasket." It was basically church oriented and led by leaders of tremendous resourcefulness such as Jesse Jackson in Chicago, Bill Jones in New York, Andrew Brown in Indianapolis, and many whose names we have not heard. It is now called PUSH, People United to Save Humanity.

The heroic struggle for open housing in Cairo, Illinois, was led by a black preacher.

One of the most powerful movements among us has been that of the Pullman-car porters once led by that venerable statesman, A. Phillip Randolph. For many years, they had no place to meet but the black church and a few lodge halls. I think they would testify to the power of the church's extended arm.

Black churches in Los Angeles, Detroit, Kansas City, Atlanta, Pittsburgh, Dallas, Cincinnati, Louisville, and in many other cities have built and are building low-cost, subsidized rental apartments, nursing homes, and apartments for the elderly. My own church, Fifth Street Baptist in Louisville, initiated and cosponsors a high-rise apartment building for the elderly known as the Blanton House.

My own involvement in the freedom-liberation movement since 1946 has been mostly with NAACP. I made a check of the officers of our branches and found that almost one third of them were black preachers. Churches across the land have taken out life memberships in the NAACP. The NAACP would have been but a ripple in the mighty waters of justice if it had not been for the black church. The organizational leaders of the NAACP have most often been churchmen: Bishop Spotswood, Gloster Current, Clarence Mitchell, Roy Wilkins. The current executive director, Benjamin Hooks, is a Baptist clergyman.

The Black Church's Outreach 137

What more could I say? We have seen the black church extending the kingdom of God in its native land through the preaching of the gospel and its worship; establishing its own publishing boards and printing its own literature; victimized because of the color and background of servitude of its members; sending missionaries to its motherland, the West Indies, Haiti, the Bahamas, South America; rearing up prophets who are scholars like Cone, Washington, Mitchell, Roberts, Thurman, Scott, Long, Proctor, Lincoln, Jones, Smith, Shannon, Wilmore, Taylor, Walker, Mays, and Kelsey who are evangelicals of a more relevant theology and promoters with a passion!

I do not mean to glamorize or put a halo where one should not be. My desire is to do my small share of demythologizing the image of the black church given to many of us in white seminaries, popularized by a few black educators and sociologists who knew not the black Joseph, rhetoricalized by a few black militants created by the white press and who, until this day, have not done their homework in black history. It appears they have never read Carter Woodson and only certain portions of W.E.B. DuBois. If so, they would have known that the church against which their angry voices have been raised has always sought to change the externally imposed image of black persons as things to persons of infinite worth, because they are made in the image of God who liberates and reconciles all people unto Himself through Jesus Christ.

The historic function of this church is still a relevant function. Seeing the reverses facing us as symbolized by municipal, state, and national politics, black people must still be inspired to endure, to hold on, to wake up, and face the demands of the rising sun. Still faced with backlashes, polarization, and alienation, the black church is called anew as an agent of liberation, however hard or difficult it may be and however much our past oppression and humiliation causes us to rebel.

You may have difficulty understanding the cause of our rebellion at the call to be an apostle of reconciliation. I don't. When I remember my father, a grown man, calling the *children* of white folks for whom he worked who were my age, Mr. Joe and Mr. Jack; when I remember having always to go to their back door because we just didn't go to Mr. Charlie's front door; when I remember being sent to the kitchen (where the food was cooked and the dishes were washed) every time I ate at a white restaurant; when I remember a member of our draft board responding to my application for a military deferment because I was a ministerial student by presenting it thus to the chairman of that board: "Barfield, Barfield, here is a boy, a black boy, who wants to be deferred"; when I remember seeing the principal of my high school drive up to a Ford agency and the owner of that agency coming out and seeing him in that brand-new Ford saying, "Here comes Nelson. Nelson is a good nigger"; when I remember two black prostitutes being run out of town because they were caught with a prominent white lawyer who remained and maintained his prominence; when I remember blacks receiving five years in the penitentiary for stealing a sack of flour and a white man given two-years suspended sentence for killing a black man; when I remember the white "icehouse" man refusing to put a fifty-pound piece of ice in my pickup truck as he did for the whites and telling me, "Come and get it yourself, nigger boy"; when I remember streets being paved to the end of the white community and left unpaved in the total black community; when I remember seeing a postman, always white, delivering mail only in the white community—it's hard for me to be an apostle of reconciliation, but this is a commandment of our Christ, and ambassadors of reconciliation we must be. Even though times have changed, blacks with these experiences will carry that memory to the grave.

We must be the Isaiah comforting the afflicted and the Amos storming the power centers of the ungodly temples of Bethel.

Like Ebed-melech we must pull together from the dungeons of hate and despair—dug by insecure princes and kings.

Unlike Israel of old, we must sing the Lord's song in a strange and hostile land.

Without becoming victims of messianic and covenant-people complexes, we must, as did Simon of old, bear the cross of Him who died to set men free. For this is the acceptable year of the Lord, the year, the hour, the moment to preach a full-orbed gospel to the poor, the gospel to heal the brokenhearted, a gospel to deliver the captives, give sight to the blind, and set free those who are oppressed.

8
Cults in the Black Community
Emmanuel L. McCall

American sociologists of religion generally recognize three broad categories of organized religious activities. These categories were first suggested by German sociologist Ernest Troeltsch.[1]

American sociologist Milton Yinger applied this criteria to the American scene.[2] Joseph R. Washington interpreted black religious movements in light of the suggestions of Troeltsch and Yinger.[3]

Their suggestion is that religious movements begin first as *cults*. A cult is a religious group organized around a charismatic leader who provides resolution for needs, fears, or anxieties. A cult is usually localized and dissipates with its founder. If the movement continues beyond its leader's exit, it becomes a *sect*.

A *sect* is a religious movement/philosophy which follows the religious tenets of its founder (who may be dead or alive) which is no longer localized and is presided over by those faithful to the founder's teachings. Initially, they aspire for inward perfection and an enlarged fellowship. It is indifferent to government and the larger society, often taking on a persecution complex because it is the object of derision and scorn.

These men suggest that should the sect continue to grow and gain acceptance by the larger society, it then becomes a *church*. As such it ceases to be indifferent to government and society and may become a participant and a shaper of both. It is also shaped by them.

New Testament interpreters share problems with the sociological definition of *church* especially in light of biblical and theological perspectives.

Characteristics of Cults

Cults have five general characteristics:

1. They are led by a new leader who usurps authority over others.
2. They claim a new revelation different from the Bible and/or other church traditions.
3. They develop a new relationship which is used to enforce authority.
4. They claim to be the only church.
5. They develop questionable definitions about God, the Holy Spirit, Jesus, salvation, faith, and works.[4]

Cults in the black community need three basic ingredients for survival: (1) hopelessness and despair, (2) a charismatic leader, and (3) accessibility, both physical and media.

Hopelessness

Place yourself in this scenario. You are a nonwhite living in America. You have come to a metropolitan area to improve your situation after leaving a small town or rural community where mechanization, lack of industries, your own limited education, lack of skills, and the color of your skin have forced unemployment.

The only housing available is multifamily apartment units which are overcrowded, noisy, rat-and-bug infested. You have to walk up five flights of stairs to get to yours. The apartment building is ill managed by an absentee landlord, unrepaired, and generally uninhabital. You may share a two-room flat with other family members or friends or crowd your own family into cramped living quarters. So crowded is it that setting a sleeping schedule is commonplace. The bathroom may often be shared with others on your floor or unit limiting both accessibility and comfort. The discomforts caused by the living situations produce social tensions that eventually may extend into legal problems. Sickness and other misfortunes easily find their way to you and your family. Loan companies and pawn shops are abundant and lure you with promises of easy payback, but you learn the hard way: "the shark bites clean." Life seems to "bottom out." What others call depression, your culture calls the low-down feeling, "the blues." You feel so far down you have to look up to see the bottom. You are tempted to drown your sorrows with cheap wine or homemade whiskey or to get high off dope. You even try suicide, but your religious and moral inclinations tell you that none of these provide the answer. You turn on the radio, and what's this?

Hope

Do you know why this lady is smiling? God blessed her and her daughter with thousands and thousands of dollars during these hard times. Here she is at church with Rev. _____ giving her tithes and offerings on the money God blessed her with.

Send for *God's Winning Combinations for 'Hard Times'* so you can prosper and have more and more money than ever during these so-called Hard Times.

Rev. _____ will walk down the aisles looking for you during the 2:45 PM meetings and look right into your eyes and bless you.

Other pitches one might hear on black-oriented radio are:

Honey, if you are unlucky in love, if your man has run out on you for another woman, you can get him back today. Come see the Prophet. I am located at _____. Make your appointment for my blessed Holy Love Oil. Once you are anointed that man will never leave you again.

Or,

> *Will you let me* mail you a Beautiful Golden Metal . . . Prosperity Cross! It has been blessed with prayer for your spiritual, physical, and financial blessing. It's free.

or,

> Mother _____ _____ is a spiritual healer. She can tell you what is wrong before you open your mouth. After she prays for you she will also tell you your future and how to prosper.

or,

> Write for my blessed prayer cloth today. Put it on your body where the pain is and pray the prayer of faith. Immediately you will be healed.

Such pitches made with background music of familiar emotional songs of hope certainly catch the attention of the hopeless. Anything seems worth a try. The person is "off to see the Wizard." Whatever financial requirement made by the cultist is honored, even if it means borrowing, begging, or stealing.

Religious superstition makes the selling of holy oil, blessed candles, special religious jewelry, blessed prayer cloths, the "blood of Jesus," and other icons a lucrative business. Persons who purchase these items or join in plans for prosperity are most often disillusioned when the expected blessing or wealth does not come. Their misfortune is blamed on faithlessness. They are instructed to fast and pray for faith.

Occasionally, some find their way out of their economic dilemma by the positive energies inspired by hope. If their prosperity coincides with the cultic practice, it gets credited with their success. Frequently, cult leaders will fill radio time with testimonies of people who have tried their methods and had their misfortunes reversed. However, black religious lore is abundant with illustrations of "stage healings" or contrived prosperity. Some of the "healings" are on people who are part of the cult leader's staff. They have rehearsed their lines and acts well and put on a convincing performance. Some are people picked in a local setting and paid to cooperate with the "healer."

Why? Why do people fall for such religious deception? The answers are: (1) the despair of hopelessness and (2) the appeal of faith. People want to be prosperous. They believe us when we evoke sacred names and indicate God's love and concern for His people. Belief in a loving Father, but ignorance as to how He blesses, makes the field of hopelessness a fertile entree for charlatans.

Several years ago a prominent white evangelist held a week-long rally in Atlanta. During that week no more than five-hundred black people attended his crusades although the Atlanta Stadium (seating capacity: forty-seven thousand) was filled each night. On Monday after the event concluded, the evangelist and some members of his team visited the Home Mission Board. In our conversation he asked, "Why did the black community not respond to my legitimate presentation of the gospel, yet on yesterday afternoon they packed the Omni (capacity: seventeen thousand) to hear Rev. _____ ?"

Several responses were given. One was the difference in the appeal. The evangelist was laboring hard to define and describe man as a lowly sinner, based and unworthy. His only hope was salvation in Christ, which also meant *taking up his cross.*

The other preacher's audience heard a different kind of message. Dressed in his thousand-dollar suits, flashing expensive jewelry, surrounded by lavish staging, after having arrived in one of his sixteen expensive cars, he was exhibit A of the prosperity his audience wanted to see, hear, and secure. They were told to repeat "I am somebody." "God doesn't make no trash." "The God in me conquers all things: pain, poverty, loneliness, and despair."

With litanies of "Green Power" (money), that brother had mesmerized his audience. While we consider such a message pure folly in light of our understanding of the Christian gospel, to people who are hopeless, the message of the cultist is the "good news" long awaited.

Cult Methods

How does the cult leader gather his following? Most frequently the media is a point of contract for the *transitory* cultist. This is the person who moves from city to city staying only long enough to extract as much money as possible. The black-oriented newspapers are used to announce his or her coming and create an air of expectancy. Radio is also extensively used with fifteen-or thirty-minute slots. The broadcast begins with music familiar to the black religious community. Once persons begin listening or singing with it, their attention is focused. Then comes the pitch, either done by the cultist or a spokesperson with a resonant voice. The voice may be female, sexy, and soothing or a masculine baritone. The pitch begins by describing the situation of hopelessness with which the listeners readily identify. Once empathy and identification are gained, the solution of hope is offered. The punch line is always the same, "God has endowed Prophet (Rev./Sister) _____ with special powers." If you want your needs met, you must go through the cultist often described as God's only anointed messenger.

The obvious attempt is to get the listener to the services or to the cultist's base of operation. If there are services they may be held in tents, rented public facilities, or even in church houses. The service begins with arousing music, both vocal and instrumental. An aid builds up the service with singing, testimonies from those who have been helped, expectancy of what will happen when the cultist arrives, and offerings. Two or three offerings are normal in the preliminary part of the service.

Seldom is the cultist on time in the service. The audience is kept waiting while the "celebrity" is in prayer or meditation, or is returning on a delayed flight from another *important* activity. When the person arrives, great fanfare is created by the presider and the instruments (usually electric organ, piano, drums, and a horn). Spotlights focus on a well-dressed and impressive-looking person whose appearance and unusual mannerisms captivate the audience. The cultist takes charge and interplays sermonettes, admonitions, teachings, healings, blessings, selling, and offerings. The hopeless may leave with a vicarious identification with the cultist that inspires hope or may leave disillusioned. If the person has participated financially, he or she leaves certainly poorer.

All cultists are not transitory, continually moving from city to city. Some set up a base of operation and become resident.

Rev. Frederick Eikerenkoetter is illustrative. During the decade of the 1960s and 70s, the leading black religious figure outside of the black church was Rev. Ike. His is a cultic movement based on the power of positive thinking and the thirst for money.

Born in Ridgeland, South Carolina, June 1, 1935, to a mixture of Dutch, East Indies, and Black bloodlines, Ike started preaching at age fourteen. In his earlier years he was a faith healer and was transitory, moving from place to place. In 1962 he established the United Church of Jesus Christ for All People in South Carolina. Two years later he moved to Boston, Massachusetts, and established his Miracle Temple which resulted from a merger of two competing congregations. Faith healing was still the emphasis. His radio broadcasts which numbered over 1,770 by 1976, a zenith period of his activity, featured various aspects of faith healing including prayer cloths, holy oil, blessed candles, and other icons.

During the mid 1960s, his philosophy took some different turns. Whether this was due to the abundance and influence of Christian Science material in Boston, or the strength of the "positive-thinking" movement, is yet to be determined. Rev. Ike says that he was moving in this direction long before his move to Boston. By 1966 Rev. Ike had moved to New York City and established the United Church, Science of Living Institute, in New York. He still uses Box 1000, Boston, MA 02103 as one of his mailing addresses.

Rev. Ike currently operates out of the United Palace, a converted theater building (formerly Loews Palace Theater) on 175th Street at

Broadway. His Sunday 3:00 PM "Joy of Living" services draw crowds in excess of five thousand. Those who come and those who hear him via radio or television experience a curious mixture of the power of positive-thinking philosophy, methods of prosperity, and black evangelical worship. Rev. Ike says he is a preacher of positive self-image: "Christianity fails all people and black people in particular." "Mind power" is the key to overcoming poverty, sickness, or problems of any kind. "There's no devil to blame here: you are your own devil."

"Heaven, also, is here and now." "Don't wait for pie in the sky: get your pie now—with ice cream on it and a cherry on top."[6]

Rev. Ike's philosophy excludes references to self-sacrifice, moral or spiritual discipline, a life of service, sharing with the less fortunate, or Christian devotion. While Father Divine, Sweet Daddy Grace, and Prophet Jones were beneficent cult leaders and became wealthy by servicing the needs of people, such is not the case with Rev. Ike. He often says, "The best thing you can do for the poor is not to be one of them."

Through the use of clinical terms like self-awareness, negativism, mind power, and "green power," he encourages his followers to will for themselves a better life. His services contain positive-thinking exercises in which the participant repeats suggestions designed to induce affirmative feelings.

Rev. Ike has an extensive mail campaign using his monthly *action* magazine and his money letters. The magazine is full of testimonies from those who have been blessed by joining his various blessing and prosperity plans. His letters are appeals for subscription to his money schemes: A Miracle Crystal Ball, Loose My Money, Green Power Money, The Finger Snapper, and Success Ideas.

Since 1980, the Rev. Ike movement has been subdued. He is not on as many radio or television stations as in the mid 1970s. His mail-out campaigns contain more references to traditional Christian values as an approach to his philosophy. His public flamboyance is minimized with the absences of an abundance of jewelry and flashy clothes. On the Tom Snyder show September, 1981, Rev. Ike was asked about this change. His response was that people were more concerned with his substances than with his message. He said he wanted his message heard rather than a focus on things.

Others in New York and Los Angeles have varying opinions about the changed Rev. Ike. For whatever reason, Rev. Ike is not seen or heard from as much since 1980 as in earlier years.

In an interview with Randall Poe that appeared in the September, 1975, issue of *Cosmopolitan,* Dr. Samuel Proctor of the Abyssinian Baptist Church, New York, described "Rev. Ike as an evangelistic fad, 'a bogus escape' for people unwilling to take on the discipline and hard work of finding sustained answers to their problems."

Were Rev. Ike a solitary figure, it would not be so disturbing. Unfortunately, his predecessors and imitators are plenteous.[7] Those who do not achieve Rev. Ike's stature as cultists operate out of homes, offices, or small buildings.

Visits to a cultist office may take a variety of forms. The office will have degrees of splendor, religious relics, and soft lighting. The person will be unusual in dress and appearance, often visionary, mysterious and penetrating. Through a knowledge of human behaviour, individual psychology, the use of catch words or slogans, the visitor is seduced, often revealing information given back as a revelation from the cultist. Suggestions are given to help the person through the crises and hope is inspired—*for a fee.*

Other Expressions

Some groups use the hopelessness/hope motif in other ways. The power of positive-thinking cults, for example, The Hillside Chapel of Truth in Atlanta, Reverend Barbara King; or Reverend Johnnie Coleman's Christ Universal Temple, Chicago, appeal to those who are middle-class oriented but are unchallenged by other churches or are aggressively mobile. They seek a religious procedure (philosophy) to aid their mobility and class awareness. These cults make creative use of the philosophy of positive thinking and apply it to the circumstances of the black community.

The Christ Universal Temple, 8601 South State Street, Chicago, Illinois, further illustrates this movement. This movement was begun in 1955 by Rev. Johnnie Coleman. Her theology then and now is considered radical by those in the mainstream of black Christian expression.

"Christ was a 'way shower' and a great prophet, but He certainly didn't die to redeem the sins of others." "Jesus died for Jesus, not for Johnnie Coleman."[8]

"Heaven and hell to us are not places." "It's heaven when you understand how to work the laws and are able to do what Jesus says: 'I came that you might have life and have it more abundantly.' When you can have an abundance of every good thing, you're in heaven, aren't you? When you're sick and broke, that's hell."

Johnnie Coleman's version of afterlife is reincarnation in the form of other people. She believes she was an Egyptian princess in an earlier life.

This movement represents an application of the power of positive thinking to personal gain. Coleman believes that anyone can become wealthy if they learn how to train their consciousness.

"You show forth what you are aware of. If you're sick, I don't care who it is, you've got a sick consciousness, or you wouldn't be sick. If you're broke, if you don't have any money, you don't have it because of your consciousness."

Reverend Coleman's services are designed to help her followers deal with words, thoughts, images, feelings, and self-concepts. She preaches "prosperity laws" to the more than four-thousand people who assemble weekly.

Coleman was formerly a schoolteacher in Mississippi. In 1953, she attended the Unity School of Christianity, Lees Summit, Missouri.

She claims healing through the Unity approach of an incurable disease which led her into the Unity ministry.

Her detractors or clerical evaluators suggest that her ministry appeals to the vanity of people without serving their spiritual needs. Some consider it humanistic because of the emphasis on what persons can do for themselves by themselves and also because of the role assigned to God in her scheme. Others feel she does not deal responsibly with the sources and effects of realities of economics in America.

Reverend Johnnie Coleman is significant not merely because of her following but because of those whom she trains and influences. They go into other cities to establish followings such as Coleman's. Because of the remigration to the South by those who went North in earlier years, the South as well as the North will be affected by the disciples of this philosophy. Their thought patterns have produced trauma in black churches where the pastors are theologically unprepared or where the congregation is influenced by upward mobility.

Some cults develop around sociopolitical motifs. The Shrine of the Black Madonna founded by Albert Cleage of Detroit capitalizes on black hopelessness, identification with African heritage, the appeal of Pan-African Unity, and the development of black economic bases. With outlets in Atlanta, Cleveland, Houston, and Philadelphia, a quasi-Christian approach is immeshed in black consciousness and hopes of economic/political advancement.

An interesting cult using the sociopolitical/religious motif is the Hebrew Israelites—see *From Night to Sunlight* by Thomas Whitfield (Nashville: Broadman Press, 1980). Internationally headquartered at 2766 Northwest 62nd street, Miami, Florida, 33147, this group has Temples of Yahweh in twenty major cities. Each temple is presided over by an "elder" with a Hebrew name: Dan Israel, Isaiah Israel, Judah Israel. Their meetings are held every Wednesday at 8:00 PM and Saturday at 9:00 AM

An illustration of how the social/political/religious theme is interwoven comes from one of their newsletters.

Blacks Must Buy Silver & Gold - Quick

The Silver is mine, and the gold is mine, saith the Lord [Yahweh] of hosts (Hag. 2:8).

O my people, we must know all truth in order to be free (John 8:33). We have been miseducated to believe that the earth and its wealth belongs to white people. Can you see that the white man's world is falling apart? *Their so-called paper money is worthless* [italics-theirs]. *Our great good and terrible black God Yahweh* is here to wake us up to reality.

Sooner or later our poor blind, deaf, dumb, ignorant and dead people will *Wake Up* and catch on and then the dollars will become absolutely worthless. Every paper currency in the world is an IOU worthless currency. None of these currencies will be freely redeemable in silver or gold. *I Warn you my people—stop accumulating paper dollars. The name of the game is to accumulate silver and gold. Silver and gold never defaults. Silver and gold has proven throughout all history to be the best store of value.*

The Yahweh newsletters are placed in residential mail boxes regularly. They contain such themes as: "Celebrate the Black Man's Holidays" (Feast of Weeks, Feast of Tabernacles, Feast of Unleavened Bread); "Yahweh's three million manufacturing plant;" "Yahweh's Judgment on America." The content of these newsletters has a similar theme, the identification of black people as the Old Testament's chosen people, condemnation of America for its treatment of black people, and the call to respond to the Yahweh movement for safety and prosperity.

It remains to be seen how the several separate attempts (Miami, New York, and Chicago) at establishing Black Hebrew followings will respond to the rebuff of April 14, 1984, when the nation of Israel refused to recognize over a thousand black Americans who had renounced their citizenship and moved to Israel. These had settled in southern Israel following the expiration of their three-month visas.

They have no rabbical connection to Judaism and no status as Americans.

Many of these "want to come home" to America. They are not only homesick but disillusioned with the movement and alienated by the Israelites.

This group of expatriots led by Ben Ami Carter are not to be confused with the Yahweh group of Miami. The point of reference has to do with religious acceptance or rejection. No different is the rejection of Hebrew blacks from the rejection of other blacks.[9]

Some cults become communes where the adherents invest their finances and labors in return for various securities (residence, food, clothes, health care, etc.) offered by the cult. The cult (more often its leader) becomes the owner of farms, restaurants, dry cleaners, stores, or other businesses.

Elder James Robert Chambers gathered the Perfect Church in Atlanta around passages in 1 John 3:8-9 and Matthew 5:48 which speaks to matters of spiritual and moral perfection. The adherents automatically "ceased sinning" and became "perfect." During his daily broadcast, his "angels" would testify of the changes in their lives since they found the "perfect way." Chambers amassed farms, several restaurants, dry-cleaning establishments, grocery stores, bakery, and a tailoring shop by the efforts of his followers. By 1983 their annual income exceeded $2 million annually.

While Chambers was alive, he was the sole officer for his "church." Following his death in September, 1983, Rev. Ron Williams, an assistant to Chambers, took over as leader. A three-man board of directors now run the movement. The emphases on "perfection" is now toned down, and the economic concerns are prominent.

The Nation of Islam and the American Muslim Mission

An illustration of another religious phenomena in the black community is the American Muslim Mission and the Nation of Islam.

These are two movements begun as a singular movement in 1930. On July 4, 1930, W. D. Farad (sometimes spelled Fard) appeared at a Fourth of July picnic in Detroit. After gathering a crowd, he proclaimed that he was a prophet of Allah and was sent to wake up the Lost/Found Nation in the West. He declared black people as inheritors of the Islamic faith and called them back to their "true destiny." Capitalizing on the social injustices which many had received from living in the South and later the North, Farad characterized whites as enemies and as "blue-eyed devils." Blacks were called to disassociate themselves from whites, from participation in political processes, to give up their slave names and take Arabic ones, to accept Islamic life-styles, and prepare for separate nationhood.

Among those influenced by Farad was Elijah Poole. Poole was originally from Sandersville, Georgia. He knew firsthand the injustices and racism to which blacks were subjected. He also knew that the North had not been the "promised land" many had expected. Poole was the son of a Baptist preacher and because of his own disenchantment with Christianity, he was open to the religion Farad was proclaiming. Poole adopted the Muslim faith, changed his name to Elijah Muhammad, and became a trusted leader of the movement. Farad sent him to Chicago to continue the movement. There Muhammad attracted a following that surpassed Farad's in Detroit.

In 1934 W. D. Farad vanished as suddenly as he had appeared four years earlier. Elijah Muhammad accepted leadership of the movement and continued until his death in February, 1975. During his lifetime, the movement took on a character that could be succinctly described as follows:

1. It is an Islamic cult dedicated to black revolution.
2. . . . antiwhite and problack
3. It emphasized black economic development by amassing businesses, restaurants, international merchandising, and farming.

Despite his antiwhite position, Muhammad drew freely upon white expertise in developing his businesses.
4. His movement had definite social reformation agenda. It accepted drug addicts, alcoholics, prostitutes, pimps, prisoners, and all who were considered as societal rejects. These he reformed into devout, religious adherents.

One of the outstanding adherents was Malcolm X. Malcolm was an articulate spokesman who used the media on Elijah's behalf as his representative. From 1954 he led the New York City movement. Malcolm could speak with fiery eloquence that attracted many young blacks looking for someone to articulate their heartbeats during the turbulent 1960s.

Malcolm maintained this preeminence until December 1, 1963. In a speech delivered in New York City, he referred to President Kennedy's assasination as "the chickens coming home to roost." Elijah silenced him for ninety days, but Malcolm saw this as an attempt by his detractors to remove him. He left the movement to start his own.

But there was simultaneously another current moving in him. Having made several trips to Mecca, the Islamic holy city in Arabia, he discovered the great discrepancies between Elijah's teachings and that of the true Islamic faith. The discrepancies made the Nation of Islam appear to be a misguided, misdirected sect of Islam which violated the spirit and purpose of the original founder. Malcolm attempted to reform the Nation of Islam in light of his newfound information. Consequently he was assassinated February 21, 1965, supposedly by one in the movement.

Replacing Malcolm as Elijah's public voice was Louis Abdul Farrakhan (sometimes Farakan). Farrakhan remained as Elijah's public voice until the leader's death in 1975.

Following Elijah Muhammad's death, one of his sons Wallace (Warith) Deen Muhammad accepted the leadership of the movement. He, too, had been to Mecca on pilgrimages and, like Malcolm X, was disappointed by the discrepancies he saw. He immediately set about the reformation of the movement. The reformation saw periodic name changes from the Nation of Islam, to Bilalians, to the World Community of Al Islam, to American Muslim Mission. The term *Bilalian* was used honoring Bilal, a muzzien (horn blower for prayer times) of the Prophet Muhammad, the original founder of the Islamic faith. The "World Community of Al Islam" represented Wallace's attempt to change from a black revolutionary sect to that embracing all Muslims. Color bars were dropped, whites and others were encouraged to join them. Any Moslem true to Prophet Muhammad's teachings could feel at ease among them. The "American Muslim Mission" represents the movement's present character as just that, an outreach of the Islamic faith in America.

Many of Elijah Muhammad's followers could not embrace the changes Wallace introduced. While most of the group subscribed to the new directions since 1978, a segment holding on to Elijah's views have been led by Louis Farrakhan. Competition among these factions continue. Even so, other modifications can be seen in Farrakhan's movement. During the 1984 presidential race, he broke with Elijah's traditions and entered the political arena by endorsing and campaigning for Jesse Jackson. Farrakhan is perceived by some as dangerous, controversial, and lunatic. Others see him as an articulate spokesman of blacks frustrated by the American system of racism. His media pronouncements caused Jesse Jackson to repudiate his support. At this writing it is uncertain what Farrakhan's future and that of the Nation of Islam may be.

The American Muslim Mission led by Warith Deen (Wallace) Muhammad and a national council of imams (ministers) continues as an American base of the Islamic faith. Says Warith of his father's movement:

> I have made a rational study of the teachings of Dr. Fard Muhammad. The one that my father said was God in person. I have done a

rational study of his teachings, and I have come to the conclusion—not today, yesterday—that the man didn't like the kind of things that he was saying and doing, but he felt that the kinds of things he was saying and doing were the only things that the ignorant, downtrodden, hopeless Bilalians in the slums of Detroit and Chicago would listen to.[10]

How true this is of most of the religious deviations in the black community.

How Shall We Respond?

A simple "anti" response to individual cult movements is counterproductive. Being against something or someone without dealing with the root of the problem resolves nothing. Since many cults operate on the hopelessness/hope motif, a Christian response is to deal with those forces causing hopelessness. Job training for the unemployed and underemployed, a direct assault on systems of injustice which prey upon people (absentee landlords, loan sharks, slum housing, incompetent court lawyers, judicial graft, inept police and justice systems, and so forth) should be a priority of churches and church organizations. Some will counter that the task of the church is *only* evangelism. The New Testament repeatedly indicates that the church has priorities in missions and ministries. One cannot read Jesus' Sermon on the Mount (Matthew 5—7) or His inaugural sermon (Luke 4:18-21) and miss His emphases on ministry. The objectives of His ministry cannot be "spiritulized" or explained away. Those who are evangelized in our churches must be discipled to accept Jesus' ministry as their own. The people who can affect change in the public and private sectors are in our churches. We must challenge and equip them for their mission.

Educational awareness of specific cult groups in its community should be a priority for any congregation. Training in interfaith witness skills will help one research and understand cult movements. To pretend that such groups are no threat or should be ignored is an inappropriate response. They will not "just go away" unless we diminish the supply line upon which they thrive. Churches might do well to have a person or committee that periodically addresses issues on religious deviations and makes reports to the congregations. Associations might do the same.

A final thing we can do is to equip pastors and church leaders with adequate knowledge of New Testament doctrines and practices so that they can respond to questions of faith raised in our congregational activities. Inquisitive persons or those having needs will go where answers can be found. Scripturally sound church leaders will provide adequate response to legitimate queries of faith. This also fills the command of our Lord to teach them "to observe all things whatsoever I have commanded you" (Matt. 28:20).

Additional Reading on Black Cults

C. Eric Lincoln, *The Black Experience in Religion* (New York: Doubleday, 1974).

Joseph R. Washington, *Black Sects & Cults* (New York: Doubleday, 1972).

H. Beecher Hicks, *Images of the Black Preacher* (Valley Forge, Pa.: Judson Press, 1977).

Gayraud Wilmore, *Black Religion & Black Radicalism* (New York: Doubleday, 1972, rev., 1973).

Arthur Faucett, *Black Gods of the Metropolis* (Philadelphia: University of PA Press, 1944).

John Henrik Clark, *Malcolm X* (Toronto, Canada: Collier Books, 1969).

Muhammad, Elijah, *Message To The Black Man in America*, n.p., n.d.

Notes

1. Ernest Troeltsch, *The Social Teachings of Christian Churches* (New York: Macmillan & Co., 1932), n. p. n.

2. J. Milton Yinger, *Religion in the Struggle for Power* (Durham, N.C.: Duke University Press, 1946), n. p. n.

3. Joseph Washington, *Black Sects and Cults* (Garden City, N. Y.: Doubleday and Co., 1972), n. p. n.

4. Information provided by Dr. Gary Leazer.

5. These quotes are from promotional materials supplied by actual cults themselves. It is easy to get on one of their mailing lists. Often, only an inquiry or small contribution is sufficient.

6. Quoted by Russell Chandler in *The Los Angeles Times,* 3 Mar., 1976.

7. Besides attendance at his services, copious listening to his broadcast tapes, and serious reading of his printed materials, the author is grateful to Clayton Riley for his article, "The Golden Gospel of Reverend Ike," *The New York Times,* 9 Mar., 1975, to Russell Chandler for, "Rev. Ike Preaches Giving Is Good—When It's to Him," *The Los Angeles Times,* 3 Mar., 1976, and to Randall Poe for, "The Reverend Ike," *Cosmopolitan,* Sept. 1975.

8. I am indebted to Lillian Williams in "Making a Place for Herself," in *The Chicago Sun-Times,* 13 Nov., 1981, for more information on this movement.

9. *The New York Times,* 15 April, 1984.

10. Warith Deen Muhammad, *As the Light Shineth from the East* (Chicago: WDM Publishing Co., 1980), n. p. n.

9
The Black Church Renaissance
Otis Moss, Jr.

(Editor's note: This chapter by Otis Moss was written in 1971, a time when the American scene witnessed various kinds of "revolutionary" action. Because the truths of this article are applicable today, the article has been only slightly revised.)

The Bible teaches us much about the concept of revolution. In the Gospel of Matthew, Jesus gives us this statement. "Think not that I am come to destroy the law, or the prophets: I am not come to destroy, but to fulfill" (Matt. 5:17). *The Good News Bible* translates this verse: "Do not think that I have come to do away with the Law of Moses and the teachings of the prophets. I have not come to do away with them, but to make their teachings come true."

This, really, is the meaning of revolution in a Christian context. Many of us use the Word without having an adequate theological and/or Christian understanding of it. We, therefore, run the risk of adopting other definitions of revolution which may or may not be what Christians ought to be saying when they talk about revolution.

Revolution, in a Christian sense, is the end of something, the fulfillment of something, and the beginning of something. If we want to examine the validity of any revolution from a Christian perspective, we must raise three questions:

What does the revolution bring an end to?
What does the revolution fulfill?

What does the revolution begin?

If it is simply an effort to gain a new position in an old world then it is not a revolution. This seems to be what most of us are working for. We are not trying to effect basic change, we just want to get on the staff in "Pharaoh's house." We are trying to get out of the "brickyard" and into the "palace." If you don't believe this, then watch the actions of those who are called from the "backyard" for a temporary appointment in the "palace." They sometimes change their rhetoric overnight. The folks we thought were marching with us begin to tell us how "you don't understand it."

"Excuse me, Brother, but I thought you were in the picket line on yesterday."

"Oh, but now is the time to change our strategy."

The challenge here is to reexamine what we really mean. Do we want a new world, or do we just want a new position in the old world?

What does the revolution we are involved in bring an end to? What does it fulfill? What does it start?

Some years ago there appeared an interesting and dynamic little book under the caption, *The Creative Revolution of Jesus: Then and Now.* Among other things, Kirby Page said that anyone who wants to understand the ministry of Jesus must be a student of revolution, for it was said by one of the contemporaries of Jesus that He wrought the most stupendous of revolutions. So if you want a revolution, start with Jesus. That's why some folk don't want Jesus. Richard Niebuhr said, "We want a Christ without a cross, a church without discipline, a God without wrath, a kingdom without judgment." But you can't have this and have revolution at the same time.

The revolution of Jesus brought an end, in one sense, to Hebraic and Pharisaic legalism. It fulfilled the prophecy, and it started a creative movement upon this earth that all men since that time must be judged by. Even when you reject Jesus you must be judged by the things that He represents.

Revolution and Growth

Revolution, then, means growth, and growth is revolution. Am I involved in the revolution? Am I growing? Jesus talks about a grain falling into the ground and dying, and in the process of dying the grain of corn protests and breaks forth out of the ground and cracks it up. A new shoot comes forth, and it grows. In the growth process it has to battle against the rain, the storm, and the sun while needing all of these at the same time. You must learn how to survive in the face of the thing you cannot get along without. You can't get along without the sunshine, but the sun can kill you if you are not quick. Have you ever heard of a sunstroke? You can't get along without sunlight, but the sunlight can blind you if you are not equipped to face it.

Am I a revolutionary? Am I growing? Revolution does not start from the outside. It starts from the inside, and it must be based on revelation. Some folk have announced a revolution, but they haven't had any revelation. Therefore, they are not building; they are stumbling and falling.

We stand today between the blind and the asinine. The asinine look at destruction and call it fulfillment. The blind look at growth and call it destruction. They call it destruction, because growth is painful. Try a real radical idea on your staff of deacons or trustees, and you will see how painful a good idea can be. But don't just start there. Try a new one on yourself. You shall know the truth, and the truth shall make you free, but generally the truth will make you mad before it makes you free.

Christian education must speak to the issue of revolution and must guide us into an understanding of the Christian concept of revolution.

Revolution and Redemption

Redemption is the most revolutionary thing on earth. Redemption means freedom. There is a political word today that often means salvation. We call it "liberation." But if we have our biblical understanding right, when someone starts talking to us about "liberation," we understand from a biblical and a theological point of view that they are talking about salvation. Don't let them upset you. You have something to tell them. You have a story to tell. Liberation means deliverance. Salvation means deliverance. It is the concept of freedom. If we have a revolution, what is the ending? What is it fulfilling? What is it beginning? If you have been converted, something ended in you. If you have been born again, something was fulfilled in you. Something is being fulfilled in you. If you have been born again, something new in you got started.

I agree with E. Stanley Jones when he says that when a man is converted, his vocabulary ought to be converted. You ought to have a new vocabulary. This is another way of saying that if you have been born again, you ought to have some new words.

When I was twelve years old, I was a water boy at a Georgia sawmill. Interestingly enough, all the language in the ghetto that we now call radical language was being used around those woods at the sawmill. Nobody wrote it down then. Even though it was not written down, one of the qualifications, I think, for holding on and holding out at the sawmill was to know how to say it real good. Now they weren't really cursing; they cussed. It was interesting enough at age twelve to get by without that kind of qualification, but you had to learn pretty fast.

There was one thing that I learned in that experience. The boss man and the owner of the sawmill would walk around with a gun on his hip. He was really running a slave camp, a concentration camp. Because he recognized that his system was unjust, he carried with him that kind of equipment because he didn't know when a rebellion might get started, or the idea might be put forth. So he had to be equipped to defend his injustice.

There was one worker whom they called "Speedy." They called him Speedy because he couldn't walk fast. He had bad feet. Speedy knew how to curse. He would curse all week long. Every time a tree fell wrong he would curse the tree out. The thing that I noticed was that it didn't matter how much he cursed the tree; it had no impact on the boss man. It didn't change his attitudes or any of our circumstances. While bad language made Speedy a big man among the workers, he was a failure in effecting change.

We can't stand in the "stables of Pharaoh" and curse our way to the "promised land." Somebody needs to inform all of us that cursing is wrong. We can stand on 125th Street in Harlem and cuss all day long, and we won't affect the Dow Jones industrial averages at all.

Some people have confused what they call militant language with militant action. Cussing is not really radical. The stock market won't change because you call a man some vulgar name. Nine times out of ten his wife called him that before you did. So don't feel that you have contributed to the revolution simply by calling some man a "pig." There is nothing revolutionary about that, but if you get hung up on that, you will end up looking like and acting like a pig yourself. It was an atheist who said, "When you deal with a monster, beware lest you become a monster."

You see, if you fight with a skunk, at close range on the ground, at his level, you will end up smelling like one, and when you walk down the streets of life, the very odor from your body will spread the news that a skunk is in town. People will get confused on what you smell like and on what you are.

When a child is bitten by a rattlesnake, we don't help the child by cursing the snake. We help the child by dealing with the wound and by coming to grips with the nature of the rattlesnake. You don't deal with a rattlesnake by crawling. We deal with a rattlesnake by being men. We don't deal with a rattlesnake by merely using the language of frustration. We have confused the language of frustration with the language of liberation. We think we are being radical and militant, but we are expressing our own frustration.

Quite often when we get so mean and so bad, we don't end up intimidating anybody but each other. Some folk look so mean and bad. They even come to meetings and hang around the walls and look. They won't smile or say anything, just look mean and bad. They are trying to intimidate, but they have not yet dealt positively with the issue.

Eighty percent of the guns that black folk buy are used to shoot other black folk. One of the techniques of the slave master has always been to put outmoded guns in the hands of slaves, in order that the slaves might shoot each other and keep themselves busy shooting each other while the slave master remained in control. One of the key instruments of the slave trade was firearms.

There were three passages in the slave trade: the outward passage, the middle passage, and the homeward passage. The outward passage can be illustrated by a ship leaving England with rum, cheap cloth, beads, and firearms. They went to the coasts of West Africa and exchanged the firearms, the rum, and the cheap beads for black cargo, human beings.

The middle passage was when they stopped at the islands and coasts of North and South America and exchanged the human cargo for sugar, cotton, and tobacco, and then began the homeward passage. We are the children of the middle passage. The slave master gave the coastal kings and some of the tribal chiefs guns and rum. Some of us now have .38s that haven't been greased good, and we are crying "revolution." We've got a .38 in one pocket and dope in the other pocket. Now that vetoes the possibility of even using the rusty .38. You don't have much target practice to start with; then when you get high on dope, you shoot everybody but the enemy. But even if the gun had been in good shape, remember that the gun is still the instrument of the slave master. So violence is the most conservative form of initiating social change.

When some people say to me "nonviolence is impractical," I know then that we have fallen short in interpreting the meaning of nonviolence. When we speak about nonviolence to the average young person, they think we're talking about going out into the streets, leaning over and putting our heads in front of a policeman's billy club, and letting him split our heads wide open, and then we come back home bloody, talking about how we've been nonviolent. That is not necessarily nonviolence.

Nonviolence begins at home. How does a father relate to his children? How does a husband relate to his wife? How does a mother relate to her family? Nonviolence begins at home. That is the responsibility that is upon our shoulders as Christians.

We must give the right interpretations. Sometimes I hear people say, "But Brother Preacher, that's dangerous." Of course it is dangerous. So is an automobile. How many people got killed in automobiles last year? Many more people got killed driving their automobiles with a license than people practicing nonviolence.

You will hear that "nonviolence is dangerous; it will get you hurt." So can a cigarette. Now, you meditate on that.

Revolution and Freedom

Not only must we know the meaning of revolution, we must also know the meaning of freedom. Freedom means to be released from something, endowed with something, and related to something. If we release a man without any endowment, he is still a slave. If you don't believe that, you get released from your husband or wife or parents with nowhere to go, nowhere to live, no money, no friends, no allies, and see how free you are. If we are going to be released from bondage, we must be endowed with something to maintain our liberty. Otherwise, we might start looking back to Egypt. Like the children of Israel of old, we will complain about being brought out into a wilderness and wishing we were back in Egypt as slaves.

We must not only be endowed with something (this is the whole history of the period called reconstruction), but we must also be related to something. We must be related to God and to our fellowman; endowed with dignity and a reasonable portion of instruments that will enable us to have some degree of self-respect and self-determination.

Not only does revelation bring an end to something and the fulfillment of something and the beginning of something. Not only does the revolution concern itself with freedom, but the revolution is a conversion experience in a special way. It means that we ought to know the difference between symbols and substance. The cross is a symbol, and I have some attachments to it. I don't mean in a sentimental way. If I confuse the symbol with the substance, I will end up worshiping the cross without knowing Jesus. The cross is a symbol. Jesus Christ is the substance. We must know the difference between symbol and substance. It is the business of Christian education to keep before us an eternal distinction between symbol and substance.

You see, this hair style which I have (an Afro) is a symbol, but what I have *in* my head is my substance. It is really foolish to walk around with an Afro hairdo and a "processed mind" (a hair-straightening style). Now I am with the Afro, and I'll give you one reason why. It has moved us out of the "stocking cap" stage (a hair-straightening process).

That was the stage in which we tried to make our hair conform to that which was not reality. To do this we wore a stocking cap all night long. We would have been much better off had we read a book for about ten minutes. But we wore the stocking caps on our heads all night long. That stocking cap kept our hair in a certain state of being for about fifteen minutes, and we went off often with a slick empty head. Now the one thing we must not do is make a transfer from a slick empty head to a bushy empty head. I'm with the symbol, and I can talk about it because I've got one.

We need the symbol of an Afro, but do we know anything about African culture? Do we know anything about what the Hebrews learned from the African? Do we know anything about the fact that some ideas found in Hebrew writings had already existed in Egyptian literature five or six thousand years before the Hebrew people got there? Do we know anything about the fact that an Ethiopian regiment came to the rescue of King Hezekiah, and historians say that it was at that point an African regiment saved the Jewish religion? Do we know anything about how Egypt and Ethiopia shook hands and gave the world a foundation for modern science? Gave the world the hour changing? Gave the world sandals? Gave the world organized religion through the development of the priesthood? I need not take more time at this point except to again raise the question, Beneath your symbol, what is your substance? Do you know anything about the empire of Ghana? Do you know anything about the empire of Mali? the University of Timbuktu? Beneath the symbol, what is your substance?

I have an African robe at home that I bought on the streets of Lagos, Nigeria. I have an African cane that I bought from a novelty shop in Accra, Ghana. These are symbols. When I put on my robe, the garment is my symbol, but my character is my substance. Beneath the symbol what about the substance?

Some of us have the symbols of revolution but not the substance of revolution. Some of us have the symbols of Christianity but not the substance of the Savior. Revolution means that we know the difference between the symbol and the substance.

Revolution means, among other things, that we have a proper balance between love and criticism. One of the things that drives young people away from the church and from us is the fact that *we have unloving critics on the one hand and uncritical lovers on the other.* Sometimes church folk make the mistake of becoming unloving critics, and sometimes parents make the mistake of being uncritical lovers. "Whatever my child does is all right." Now we mistakingly call that love. In order to fill the emptiness at Christmas and Easter we pile upon them all kinds of material trinkets to make up for the emptiness that came when we shirked the opportunity of discipline. What we need is critical love and loving critics. If you love me critically, you can also love me tenderly. If you love me tenderly, you make me to know what I can do. If you love me critically, you let me know what I can become.

The late Dr. H. H. Coleman of Detroit said that we have trained our children in how *to get,* but we have not trained up a child in how *to go.*" "Train up a child in the way he should *go"* (Prov. 22:6, author's italics). But we have trained them in the way they should get. They know how to get everything, but they don't know how to go. They don't know how to go because *we* don't know how to go.

Revolution is a teaching experience. Revolution ought to teach the meaning of concepts, phrases, and ideas. Some folk got scared to death (more black folk than white) over simple words like "black power," without knowing what it meant. When we get a classical definition of black power, we find that it is an instrument for teaching. My definition of black power is black maturity; black maturity is economic security; economic security is political ingenuity; political ingenuity is functional ethnic unity. These must be built on books, bucks, and ballots, plus an indestructible self-appreciation and a sense of spiritual integrity.

The revolution is a teaching experience. It teaches that liberation is salvation, that freedom is redemption, that "right on" is a new "amen."

The revolution teaches that the church ought to be the focal point of radical idealism and creative realism. The church was made for the unfit, unholy, unrighteous, unworthy, and unready. The church was established to "comfort the afflicted and afflict the comfortable."

There are two necessary realities that must be present for a true revolution: love and truth. Nothing is more radical than love. Nothing is more militant and redeeming than truth. The church is the house of God only insofar as it is the house of love and the house of truth. When these realities are present in the church, we can speak with unlimited resources to everybody we meet and say: "Come and go with me to my Father's house."

10
Selected Bibliography on the Black Church

Ames, Russell. *The Story of American Folk Song.* New York: Grosset and Dunlop, 1955.

Baker, Benjamin. *Shepherding the Sheep.* Nashville: Broadman Press, 1983.

Bennett, Lerone. *What Manner of Man: A Biography of Martin Luther King, Jr.* Chicago, Il: Johnson Publishing Company, 1964.

Boesak, Allan. *Farewell to Innocence.* Maryknoll, N.Y.: Orbis Books, 1977.

Boodie, Charles E. *God's "Bad Boys."* Valley Forge, Pa.: Judson Press, 1972.

Booth, L. V. *Crowned with Glory and Honor.* Hicksville, N.Y.: Exposition Press, 1978.

Burkett, Randall. *Garveyism as a Religious Movement: The Institutionalization of a Black Civil Religion.* Metuchen, N.J.: Scarecrow Press, 1978.

Carter, Harold A. *The Prayer Tradition of Black People.* Valley Forge, Pa.: Judson Press, 1976.

Clark, Erskine. *Wrestlin' Jacob: A Portrait of Religion in the Old South.* Atlanta: John Knox Press, 1979.

Cone, Cecil. *The Identity Crisis in Black Theology.* Nashville: AMEC, 1975.

Cone, James. *Black Theology and Black Power.* New York: Seabury Press, 1969.

Cone, James. *The Spirituals and the Blues.* New York: Seabury Press, 1972.
Cone, James. *My Soul Looks Back.* Nashville: Abingdon Press, 1982.
Cone, James. *For My People.* Maryknoll, N.Y.: Orbis Books, 1984.
Day, Richard Ellsworth. *Rhapsody in Black: The Life Story of John Jasper.* Valley Forge, Pa.: Judson Press, 1953.
Dorough, C. Dwight. *The Bible Belt Mystique.* Philadelphia, Pa.: West Minster, 1974.
George, Carol V. R. *Segregated Sabbaths: Richard Allen and the Rise of Independent Black Churches.* London: Oxford University Press, 1973.
Hicks, H. Beecher, *Images of the Black Preacher.* Valley Forge, Pa.: Judson Press, 1977.
Hill, Samuel. *Religion and the Solid South.* Nashville: Abingdon Press, 1972.
Holmes, Thomas. *Ashes for Breakfast.* Valley Forge, Pa.: Judson Press, 1969.
Jackson, J. H. *A Story of Christian Activism: History of the National Baptist Convention U.S.A., Inc.* Nashville: Townsend Press, 1980.
Johnson, James Weldon. *God's Trombones.* New York: Viking Press, 1968.
Johnson, Joseph. *The Soul of the Black Preacher.* Philadelphia: Pilgrim Press, 1971.
Jordan, Winthrop, *White Over Black.* Baltimore: Penquin Books, 1968.
King, D. E. *Preaching to Preachers.* Warminster, Pa.: Neibauer Press, 1984.
King, Martin Luther, Jr. *Stride Toward Freedom.* New York: Harper & Row, 1958.
Lincoln, C. E. *Martin Luther King, Jr.* New York: Hill and Wang Press, 1970.
Lofton, Fred. *When We Pray.* Elgin, Ill.: Progressive Baptist Publishing House, 1978.

Selected Bibliography on the Black Church 173

Massey, James. *The Responsible Pulpit.* Anderson, Ind.: Warner Press, 1974.

Mays, Benjamin. *Disturbed About Man.* Richmond, Va.: John Knox Press, 1969.

Mays, Benjamin. *Born to Rebel.* New York: Charles Scribner's Sons, 1971.

Mbiti, John. *The Prayers of African Religion.* Maryknoll, N.Y.: Orbis Books, 1975.

McKinney, Samuel and Massey, Floyd. *Church Administration in the Black Perspective.* Valley Forge, Pa.: Judson Press, 1976.

Mitchell, Henry. *Black Preaching.* New York: Lippincott Company, 1970.

Mitchell, Henry. *Black Beliefs.* New York: Harper & Row, 1975.

Mitchell, Henry. *The Recovery of Preaching.* New York: Harper & Row, 1979.

Muhammed, Warith. *As the Light Shineth from the East.* Chicago, Ill.: WDM Publishing Company, 1980.

Odum, Howard and Johnson, Guy. *The Negro and His Songs.* New York: New American Library, 1925.

Owens, J. Garfield. *All God's Chillun.* Nashville: Abingdon Press, 1971.

Peterson, Thomas. *Ham and Jopheth.* Metuchen, N.J.: Scarecrow Press, 1978.

Philpot, William. *Best Black Sermons.* Valley Forge, Pa.: Judson Press, 1972.

Ray, Sandy. *Journeying Through a Jungle.* Nashville: Broadman Press, 1979.

Roberts, J. Deotis. *Roots of a Black Future.* Philadelphia: West Minster, 1980.

Sernett, Milton. *Black Religion and American Evangelicalism.* Metuchen, N.J.: Scarecrow Press, 1975.

Smith, J. Alfred. *Outstanding Black Sermons.* Valley Forge, Pa.: Judson Press, 1976.

Smith, J. Alfred. *For the Facing of this Hour.* Elgin, Ill.: Progressive Baptist Publishing House, 1981.

Smith, J. Alfred. *Preach On.* Nashville: Broadman Press, 1984.

Smith, J. Alfred. *The Informed and Growing Trustee.* Oakland, Calif.: Allen Temple Baptist Church, 1984.

Smith, H. Shelton. *In His Image, But: Racism in Southern Religion* Durham, N.C.: Duke University Press, 1972.

Smitherman, Geneva. *Talkin and Testifyin: The Language of Black America.* Boston, Mass.: Houghton Mifflin Company, 1977.

Sullivan, Leon, *Build Brother Build.* Philadelphia: Macrae Smith Company, 1969.

Taylor, Gardner. *How Shall They Preach?* Elgin, Ill.: Progressive Baptist Publishing House, 1977.

Taylor, Gardner. *The Scarlet Thread.* Elgin, Ill.: Progressive Baptist Publishing House, 1981.

Thurman, Howard. *The Luminous Darkness.* New York: Harper & Row, 1965.

Walker, Wyatt. *Somebody's Calling My Name.* Valley Forge, Pa.: Judson Press, 1979.

Wilmore, Gayraud. *Black Religion and Black Radicalism.* Maryknoll, N.Y.: Orbis Books, 1983.

Wilmore, Gayraud and Cone, James. *Black Theology.* Maryknoll, N.Y. Orbis Books, 1979.

Woodson, Carter. *The History of the Negro Church.* Washington, D.C.: Associated Publishers, 1921.

About the Authors

Dr. Ella P. Mitchell serves with her husband, Dr. Henry H. Mitchell at Virginia Union Theological Seminary, Richmond, Virginia. She holds an earned Th.D. from Claremont School of Theology.

Dr. Henry H. Mitchell is a prolific writer on preaching in the black tradition. He has served on the faculties of California State University, Colgate Rochester Divinity School, North Carolina Central University. Currently he is Dean at Virginia Union Theological Seminary, Richmond.

Dr. W.J. Hodge has been Pastor of the Fifth Street Baptist Church, Louisville, Kentucky, since 1957. He is also president of Simmons Bible College. Hodge has been very active in the struggle for justice and has been a leader in the NAACP in Kentucky.

Dr. Otis Moss is pastor of the Olivet Institutional Baptist Church, Cleveland, Ohio. He has been very active in the justice struggles across the nation. Moss is a very popular speaker in revivals and other religious convocations.

Dr. Dearing E. King recently retired as pastor of the Monumental Baptist Church, Chicago, Illinois. He also served the Zion Baptist

Church, Louisville, Kentucky, for a number of years. King is internationally famous for his gifts as a liturgist.

Dr. Wendell P. Whalum has been on the faculty of Morehouse College since 1953. He has and continues to serve as organist and choirmaster for prestigious churches in the Atlanta area. Whalum is famous for the Morehouse College Glee Club which has national and international renown.

Dr. Emmanuel McCall has served on the staff of the Home Mission Board of the Southern Baptist Convention since 1968. Currently he is director of the Black Church Relations Department, and has been coordinator of Black Church Studies at the Southern Baptist Theological Seminary, Louisville, Kentucky, since 1970.